The Great Wood
of Caledon

First published in Great Britain by
Colin Baxter Photography Ltd.,
Unit 2/3, Block 6,
Caldwellside Industrial Estate,
LANARK, ML11 6SR

British Library Cataloguing in Publication Data
Miles, Hugh
    The great wood of Caledon.
    1. Scotland. Woodlands
    I. Title II. Jackman, Brian
    914.1104859

    ISBN 0-948661-26-7

Illustrations © Keith Brockie 1991

Photography:

© Laurie Campbell 1991:
Front Cover, Back Cover and Pages 12, 13, 16, 17, 23, 28 (all 4), 31,
34, 35, 36, 37, 38, 44, 45, 54, 55, 56, 65, 68, 69, 74, 77, 78, 79, 81,
86, 87, 90 (all 4), 91, 92, 93, 98, 99, 100, 101, 111.

© Colin Baxter 1991:
Endpapers and Pages 6, 14, 15, 19, 41, 49, 61, 71, 83, 95, 103, 106,
107, 108, 109.

© Mike Read 1991:
Pages 22, 26, 29, 39, 52, 64, 75.

© Michael W. Richards 1991:
Pages 53, 57.

© Hugh Miles 1991:
Page 76.

Map by Oxford Illustrators Ltd based on McVean/Ratcliffe:
Plant Communities of the Scottish Highlands, Crown copyright.
Used with permission from HMSO.

Printed in Great Britain by
Frank Peters (Printers) Ltd., Kendal.

The Great Wood of Caledon

Hugh Miles
&
Brian Jackman

Colin Baxter Photography Ltd., Lanark, Scotland.

The Great Wood of Caledon

Our Special Thanks

I first visited the Highlands thirty years ago, and coming from the flat fen country it was hardly surprising that I fell under the spell of Scotland's beautiful glens and spectacular wildlife. For five years I filmed there for the Royal Society for the Protection of Birds, and it was at this time that I met Brian, who was writing about the plight of the Caledonian pine forests for *The Sunday Times*. We forged a friendship and a working relationship that continues to this day.

More recently, I was able to fulfil a long-held ambition to make a film about the forests. The film took three years to make, during which time the Highlands became my second home, where Brian joined me whenever possible. Out of these shared experiences this book was born, in the hope that others too can share in this celebration of Caledon's continued existence, its sheer beauty and its great antiquity.

Walking in the forest is a privilege that no one can take for granted, and would not have been possible without the kindness and generosity of landowners, wardens and keepers throughout Scotland, many of whom we are now fortunate to count as friends. First among these are Stewart and Janet Taylor and the many RSPB staff who gave so freely and generously of their time, expertise and encouragement. Roy and Marina Dennis were always at hand and supportive despite hectic schedules, and Dick Balharry and his many colleagues in the Nature Conservancy Council were endlessly helpful. Our demanding wildcats received the dedicated care of Jo and Mollie Porter, who also helped in many other ways; to them a big thank you. We should also like to thank the numerous scientists, foresters and conservationists who combed our manuscript for inaccuracies; if errors have crept in despite their efforts, they are entirely ours. We had the privilege and pleasure of working with Adam Watson on the film, and only wish that we had shared more time with him among his beloved pines.

Special thanks to our loyal colleagues in the field who spent so many weeks with us, including Mike Read and Mike Richards, who also supplied a few of the photographs; and above all to Torquil and Jean McIntyre, who provided a home and a welcome and were an endless source of kindness and encouragement.

Christine Launder's patience and accuracy in typing the manuscript were impressive, and Keith Brockie, Colin Baxter and Laurie Campbell laboured long and hard to produce the evocative images of the forest and its wildlife. I am sure they share the wish that our joint efforts are a way of saying 'thank you' to the many who have contributed to this book.

If reading about the ancient forests contributes to your understanding and concern, then we have achieved our aim. If you are encouraged to care enough, then make a contribution to the RSPB or the Scottish Wildlife Trust, or better still, become a member and contribute to the lasting protection of wildlife and wild places.

Royal Society for the Protection of Birds
The Lodge
Sandy
Bedfordshire
SG19 2DL

Scottish Wildlife Trust
25 Johnston Terrace
Edinburgh
EH1 2NH

If you visit the forest please tread silently; then you too will experience the magic of the Great Wood and hear the echoes of ancient Caledonia.

Hugh Miles
Corfe Mullen
Dorset

The Great Wood of Caledon

Contents

For Stewart and Janet Taylor, who have given so much to the forest

Loch Shin

Glen Einig

Rhidorroch

Amat

Strath Vaich

Loch Maree

Coulin

Shieldaig

Achnashellach

Glen Strathfarrar

Glen Cannich

Glen Affric

Loch Ness

Dalnahaitnach

Strathspey

Abernethy

Guisachan and Cougie

Glenmore

Glen Moriston

Glen Avon

Glen Loyne

Rothiemurchus

Glen Quoich

Barisdale

Glengarry

Glen Derry

Loch Arkaig and
Glen Mallie

Great Glen

Glen Feshie

Ballochbuie

Glen Loy

Mar

Ardgour

Glen Nevis

Loch Rannoch

Black Wood of Rannoch

Black Mount

Meggernie

Loch Tay

Glen Orchy

Tyndrum

Glen Falloch

Loch Lomond

0   30 miles

0   50 kms

Former distribution of native
Scots pine forests

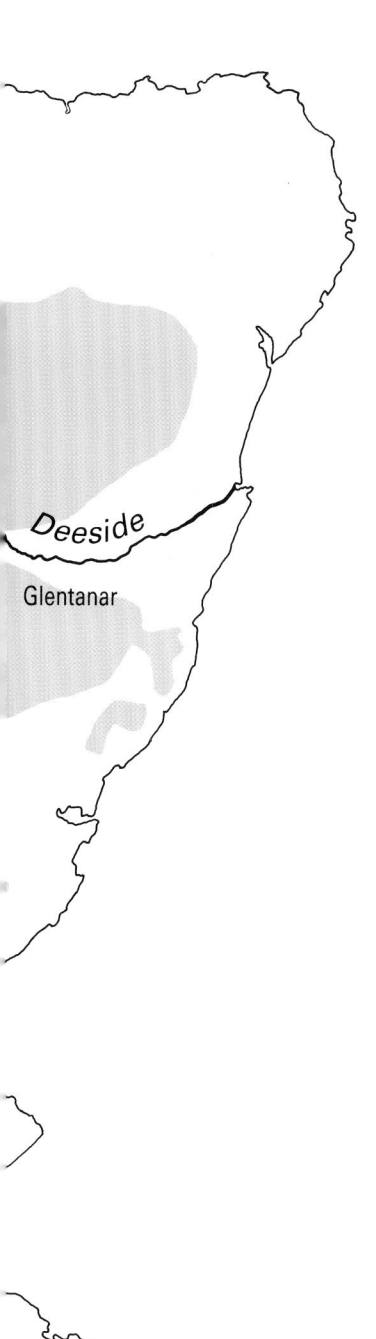

Present-day remnants of native
Scots pine forests

Deeside

Glentanar

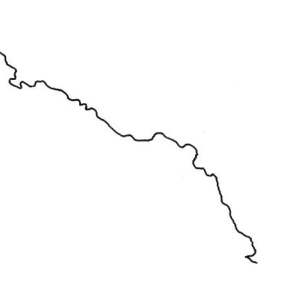

The Great Wood of Caledon

The ancient pinewoods of Scotland are among the most important living historical monuments in Britain and Europe. Largely unmodified by man, the native forests are the descendants of those of early post-glacial times and had been growing for several millennia when Ptolemy first used the name Caledonian Forest in the second century AD. Their future has been a cause for concern for centuries. During the 1975 symposium on the Native Pinewoods, A. Carlisle, co-author of the definitive book on the subject, summarised the history of man's impact as follows:

'1. Although man has been grazing, burning and cultivating since Neolithic times, his effect on the indigenous pine forests of Scotland was probably not very great until after the Lowland forests were exhausted in the 16th and 17th-centuries and man turned to the remoter Highlands for timber.

2. The depletion of accessible Lowland woods, an increased demand for timber for building, and a growing iron industry resulted in surveys of the pine forests being made in the 16th and 17th-centuries with a view to assessing the value of these Highland forests as sources of timber.

3. The pine forests were saved from complete destruction by their inaccessibility and the consequent problems of timber extraction. However, increasing demands for timber and the improvement of timber floating techniques resulted in extensive exploitation that began in the 17th-century and continued until the middle of the 19th-century, with a peak of activity during the Napoleonic Wars. Since then there have been periods of heavy exploitation during two World Wars.

4. It does not seem likely that, at least in the larger forests, the Scots pine gene pool has been greatly depleted. Some small pine forests have been virtually destroyed and their gene pool depleted, and the genetic purity of some forests has been threatened by planting pine of unknown or non-local origin in or adjacent to the indigenous pine forests.

5. Regeneration of the pine forest has been associated with major site disturbances by logging and fire, particularly the latter. Scots pine in the natural state appears to be partly fire dependent. The successful control of fire in recent times may be the reason for some regeneration problems we face today. Regenerating failure is also due to excessive grazing.

6. Scots pine seems to be well adapted to the relatively infertile soils of the native pinewoods. Logging and burning have probably caused a considerable loss of macronutrient elements from the soil. We do not know what these pinewood soils would be like without man's interference.

7. Since Palaeolithic times, several large mammals (elk, caribou, bear, lynx and wolf) have become extinct in Scotland, due to both man and changes in climate. Today man tends to shoot species which interfere with his recreation, agriculture, and timber production, so that populations of raptors and such pine-damaging birds as capercaillie and black grouse are probably lower than the forest can support. Some species, such as foxes and hooded crows, are very resilient to man's active hostility. Control of fox and deer populations will probably always be necessary.'

At the time of the symposium, Jean Balfour, then of the Countryside Commission for Scotland, stated:

'In 1972, the Verney Committee wrote in their report *Sinews for Survival*, "Trees are beautiful as well as useful, they are one of our country's renewable natural resources, too often they are taken for granted."

Unlike agricultural land, where man at least in northern Europe and certainly in Scotland soon learned to husband this resource by caring for the land and fostering and improving its crop, forests have been steadily exploited until the 20th-century (and, of course, in much of the world, exploitation continues at an ever faster rate). Efforts by the Scots Parliament, from as early as the 12th-century onwards by law and charter, to encourage planting and punish over-cutting, failed to prevail against the needs of fuel, building, destruction of wolves and bandits and the English attempts at conquest, with its attendant destruction. Let us at least be encouraged that today we are no longer taking them for granted.

But the great danger today is not that we take the pine forests for granted, but that, in talking about them, we forget that talk is no substitute for action. Without action, future conservationists may find much of the forest has ceased to exist.'

Let us hope that in the 1990s and beyond, the new conservation organisation 'Scottish Natural Heritage' is able to ensure that the Great Wood of Caledon lives on.

CHAPTER ONE

The Shrinking Forest

Above the high tops of the Cairngorms, where blizzards had piled the snow in deep drifts and curling cornices, an eagle was hunting. Alone among the creatures of the Scottish Highlands it appeared indifferent to the harshness of the northern winter. It flew in the teeth of the wind, dark wings outstretched, scanning the piebald slopes for the huddled shapes of hare or ptarmigan, but saw only deer moving down from the hills.

The deer were heading for the pine forest which lay in the deep-frozen silence of Strathspey. There, beside the black waters of Loch Mallachie, the great trees stood, rank on rank, solid and reassuring; a refuge not only for deer but for wildcat and pine marten, crossbill, crested tit and capercaillie. Snowflakes came whirling across the heather and clung to the thick winter manes of the leading stags as they made for the sheltering trees. Despite their heavy coats they were gaunt and rangy beasts, the product of long years in the open hills and high corries; yet their true habitat lies within the sentinel pines of Abernethy, a remnant of the Great Wood of Caledon.

Together, deer, eagle and native pine have occupied the Strath since the last Ice Age; but the Great Wood is no more. Of the million and a half hectares which once sprawled like a shaggy green pelt from Deeside to the western sea lochs, there are only scattered remnants. The deer have long since adapted to a fugitive life among the heather and peat hags of the open moors, where the Great Wood survives only in the archaic language of stalkers and keepers who still refer to these barren hillsides as 'deer forest'. In winter, when the heather lies deep under the snow and blizzards sweep down from the hills, they respond as if to some sacred lure and return to their ancestral sanctuary among the ancient pines.

The Scots pine is one of the world's most successful trees. It grows as a native species in more countries than any other conifer, extending from Scotland to China, and from the Arctic down to the high sierras of southern Spain. In Britain it was one of the first trees to arrive from the Continent after the last Ice Age. As the glaciers retreated, some 10,000 years ago, the ice was replaced by a barren tundra of moss and Arctic lichens. Crowberries ripened in the brief summers. Bog myrtle added a new pungency to the air. Thickets of juniper, dwarf birch and willow sprang up on the lower ground, and alders spread along the river valleys.

When the first trees arrived, the birth of Christ was still 6,000 years away. After the birch came the pines, and together they formed our first permanent post-glacial woodland - a boreal wilderness that echoed to the howling of wolves and the bugling of elk. The slender birch, so swift to colonize, is a short-lived tree with a life span no greater than our own. Not so the Scots pine. Bigger, tougher, altogether more durable, these hardy conifers have an average life of 150 years. Some may stand for more than 300 years - like the 395-year-old veteran of Arkaig, in Inverness-shire - and in time they became the dominant species.

No sooner had the pines established their supremacy than they faced their first real challenge. As the climate grew more temperate it encouraged a second wave of trees, which spread out in the wake of the conifers like an invading army, to seize the Welsh valleys and wide English plains. In the south, the broad-leaved oak was king; but in the cold north, on the thin sands and glacial gravels of the Highlands, the great pines remained unchallenged, lording it over the oak and the lesser trees: birch, alder, rowan and juniper.

The Great Wood of Caledon is our oldest British woodland, a primeval northern forest which had already been standing for at least 2,000 years when Stonehenge was raised on Salisbury Plain. In that prehistoric heyday the Great Wood was a mosaic of dense forest, wind-blown glades and bare bogs. There was hardly a glen that was not roofed with trees, the high hills rising like islands from the blue-green canopy. The wolf and the lynx roamed its trackless deeps. Bears and wild boars snuffled among its roots; and the ancient pines rose and fell in an endless cycle of decay and regeneration.

For centuries the Great Wood lay undisturbed. When the Romans came to Britain it became a refuge for the Pictish tribes who waged guerrilla war on the

Together, deer, eagle, and native pine have occupied the Strath since the last Ice Age.

imperial legions. In time the Romans withdrew and peace returned to the place they called "Caledon" - the wooded heights. Far to the south the Saxons arrived and carved out their English earldoms. The pines outlived them all.

Then came the Vikings, and the war on the Great Wood began. In the west they torched the forests and felled the tall trees to fashion masts for their longships. One by one, as their stronghold shrank, the forest fauna were hunted down. Brown bear, lynx and reindeer were all gone by the 10th-century; the boars and beavers lasted a few centuries more, bringing wealth to Inverness as a fur-trading port. For the Highland Scots the trees were fuel, and huge gaps appeared in the forest canopy as feuding clans burned the woods of their enemies. Yet still the Great Wood stretched for miles, a sanctuary for wolves and renegades alike until the English arrived to smoke them out.

The last wolf was killed in Inverness-shire in 1743, and two years later the crushing of Bonnie Prince Charlie's Highland rebels signalled the end of the glory of Caledon. Down came the mighty trees, felled by the impoverished clan chiefs who, forced to pay off their hated new Hanoverian landlords, sold their timber to English ironmasters.

Thereafter the Highland landowners became increasingly keen on exploiting their pinewoods. Forest giants which had stood since the Wars of the Roses were now felled and floated down-river to build ships.

Between 1780 and 1890, 300 ships were built at the mouth of the Spey from pines floated down river from the shrinking forest. At the same time entire human communities were uprooted to make way for deer and sheep. The deer multiplied, eating up the seedling pines and preventing regeneration, as they have done to this day.

*All that remains of the Great Wood are scattered remnants, which comprise
less than one per cent of the original forest cover.*

Wherever the pines make their last stand it is still possible to catch the illusion of that vanished Caledon.

in Nethy Bridge and elsewhere began clear-felling mile after splintered mile.

The destruction has continued almost to this day, and it should be a cause for national shame that the Forestry Commission destroyed half of all the genuinely native pinewoods it owned 30 years ago. Such is the tale of human folly that brought the Great Wood to its knees.

Today, less than one per cent of the original forest cover is left. All that remains of the Great Wood is barely 17,000 hectares, broken up into 35 scattered remnants of which the smallest - in Glen Falloch, Glen Loyne and Glen Avon - hold fewer than 150 trees. Centuries of clear-felling, burning and overstocking with sheep and deer have laid bare the hillsides of northern Scotland and reduced them to treeless badlands.

Fortunately, in the best surviving pockets, at Abernethy and Rothiemurchus in the shadow of the Cairngorms, on the bristling islets of Loch Maree at

Meanwhile, improvements in the efficiency of sporting guns created a demand for more grouse, giving rise to intensive keepering and a ruthless war on vermin. The Victorian craze for egg collecting and taxidermy was, in many instances, the final blow, and between them keepers and collectors helped to wipe out a whole range of spectacular predators and scavengers, among them the sea eagle, osprey, goshawk, red kite and polecat. Other species - wildcat, pine marten, hen harrier and golden eagle - were also shown little mercy, and would not recover until late into our own, more enlightened, century.

By the 1860s the axe had bitten deep into the woods of Rothiemurchus, providing sleepers for the new Highland Railway. There was no respite. Many more trees fell in the two world wars. The pines of Deeside survived the Great War, but Speyside suffered huge losses which continued during the Second World War, when Canadian lumbermen based at large camps

Being Fhigh on the west coast, in Glen Affric and the Black Wood of Rannoch - wherever the pines make their last stand, it is still possible to catch the illusion of that vanished Caledon, to sense the past reaching back through the shadowy trunks to the untouched wildwood of long ago.

There is now a greater awareness of the value of these splendid trees, not as timber but as living monuments which have no equal, a part of Scotland's heritage no less historic than its castles and palaces. The Forestry Commission no longer regards our native pines simply as a cash crop. In areas such as Glen Affric Forest - parts of which are now managed as a Caledonian pine reserve - non-native trees have been removed and deer fences erected to give the original growth a chance to regenerate. Today, all but about 15% of the surviving native pinewoods lie within national nature reserves or have been designated by the Nature Conservancy Council as sites of special scientific interest.

These old woods are hallowed places, touched with a haunting beauty. The trees are not set in gloomy regimental rows. They grow randomly, often scattered and widely spaced in a way that lets in the light and creates magical depths of space and serenity. Their shapes are wonderfully varied. Some trees are graced with drooping branches; others carry spreading crowns, like the flat-topped acacias of the African savannah. Some are gnarled and misshapen, bent double by the wind as they claw their way up the rocky hillsides to the limit of their range - 2,000 feet above

sea level. Others still grow tall and straight, reaching for the sky, not because they were planted by a forester but because they sprang up together after a forest fire opened a gap in the canopy.

There is beauty, too, in the individual tree itself, in the colours of the bark, silver-grey and flaring salmon-pink, and in its flaky texture, deeply fissured at the base of the trunk, peeling and papery on the higher branches. Even on a winter's day, in the blue-green shadows of the billowing canopy, with snow-clouds massing over the sombre hills, they seem to give out their own candescent orange glow.

The Scots pine grows to an average height of 50 feet. Just how big they become depends on the nature of their surroundings and how close they stand together, but many trees reach 70 feet and a few may rise 90 feet above the heather and blackberry. Craggy and long-living like the oak, the Scots pine has a courageous quality that suits its wild surroundings. To stand among these hoary old veterans with the snow falling and the wind moaning in the high branches is to know how northern Britain must have appeared in the wolf-winters of our prehistoric past.

Now the wolf, elk and bear are gone, but the woods still harbour many of their original wildlife species. For, like all forests, these pinewoods are not just a gathering of trees but complex associations of wild plants and creatures. Crossbill and crested tit, red squirrel and pine marten, each has its part to play in maintaining the miraculous equilibrium of the living wood.

♂ Scottish Crossbill — frosty morning

CHAPTER TWO

Parrots of the Pinewoods

The snow-covered Cairngorms glistened white behind the ancient pines. Mist drifted through the trees and mountain tops, obscuring the forest, but as the rising sun burnt moisture from the sky, the veil lifted, revealing the shadowy giants of Rothiemurchus, spreading far across the valley.

Walking into the Great Wood, there came, as always, that sense of entering hallowed ground. The air held a reverent hush, as if the ancient trees were waiting, aware perhaps that being so old they should not hurry. Standing beneath the towering giants, the forest seemed empty, the only sound being the murmuring of the age-old pines, echoing memories of centuries past. But eyes and ears became tuned to the evidence that there had been life here: holes in trees, scrapes in moss, twisted cones, a paw print in the earth. Then a sound, faint at first, but growing louder and more insistent, the call of one of Europe's rarest birds, found nowhere else in the world, the Scottish crossbill.

As it landed in the top of a tall pine, we could see that it was a male, the orange-red plumage standing out against the blue-green pine. Its sharp, strident calls attracted other crossbills, whose bounding flight carried them across a large clearing, to settle in the tree-tops above us. Some were female, the same size as the males, but with their green backs and yellowish rumps well-camouflaged for nesting in the pines. Calling excitedly, they dropped into the outer branches and started to feed.

With their exotic colours and huge, scissor-like bills, they scurried among the clustered cones like miniature parrots. Using their crossed mandibles, they are able to prise open the protective scales of unopened cones, then with extra long tongues reach down between them to extract the seeds. As we watched, the discarded wings of the seeds spiralled silently down towards us, to be overtaken by discarded cones which rattled noisily through the branches. Crossbills are always fastidious in their choice of cones and seeds, and many were rejected as they moved from tree to tree.

We were surprised to see that when the crossbills fed they broke most of the cones off the tree, carried them in their beak to a suitable branch, then held them down with one foot before splitting them open. Scots pine cones are very tough and this is thought to be the reason why Scottish crossbills, which feed on Scots pine seeds, have evolved larger bills than their spruce seed-eating relations. Originally there was only one sort of crossbill, but after the Ice Age, geographic isolation allowed differences to develop and we now have parrot crossbills in Scandinavia, the widespread common crossbill, and the Scottish crossbill, found only in these Highland forests where the Scots pine grows.

The first description of crossbills was written in 1251, when monks observed them eating apple seeds in an English monastery. Scottish crossbills are sometimes seen eating insects - even putty from crofters' windows - but their staple diet is pine seeds and this occasionally causes them serious problems.

The Scots pine has a two-year breeding cycle in which the cone represents the fruit of the tree. Pollination takes place during warm, sunny weather in May, when the small yellowish male cones, resembling miniature pineapples, burst clouds of pollen into the breeze. This blizzard of life fertilizes the tiny red female flowers, and in a year's time they grow into little green cones. By the following spring they are fully mature. Then for two or three weeks, usually during April and May, as they ripen in the spring sunshine, the protective, woody scales crack open and the winged seeds fly out, to float gently to the forest floor.

Those seeds that land in the shade of the parent tree, or other venerable giants nearby, will not do so well; but there is always a good chance of germination if they land in the open, especially if the ground has been cleared by fire or raked bare by large mammals. In the past these would have included wild boars and brown bears, but in their absence the seeds are faced with the problems of penetrating the tall, rank heather and deep peat layers, both detrimental to germination. In the west, where the wetter climate has created boggy ground cloaked with sphagnum moss, there is even less regeneration and some remnants of the forest are graveyards of dead and dying trees, sad monuments to a once great Caledonia.

The seed production of individual trees varies enormously from year to year. In a good season a mature tree may yield 3,000 cones and a huge amount of seed; in a poor year it may produce none at all. This creates problems for Scottish crossbills, but the saving grace is that productivity varies from one wood to the next; and somewhere in the Highlands there is always likely to be some ripe cones to feed the flocks.

Scottish crossbills have also learnt to take advantage of the new plantations of exotic conifers. In Sutherland, for instance, they commonly feed on Sitka spruce and Lodgepole pine, moving on to the Scots pine only when it ripens later in the season. But in the western Highlands, the extensive spruce plantations do not help Scottish crossbills, for they produce seed even less frequently than the Scots pine.

Before the planting of exotic conifers took place, the crossbills' reliance on the Scots pine for food made them very vulnerable and the drastic reduction in the total area of forest in which they could search led to a big decrease. They are now very rare, and their numbers are reduced even further during years of poor cone crops. At least one keeper we know has, on several occasions, found crossbills lying on the forest floor, starved to death.

The irregular cone crops are the reason why crossbills are so unpredictable, restlessly moving from place to place, calling loudly to keep the flock together - especially important during times of courtship. The group we were watching suddenly separated, with one pair flying off towards the mountains. Following them as best we could - at one point we had to wade through the Druie river - we found them again on a stunted pine, the male singing on the highest sprig, the female feeding below. The crossbill's song often appears ventriloquial, for it is never very loud and the throat moves more than the beak. He moved closer to the female, courting her, in a

The Scottish crossbill - found only in these Highland forests where the Scots pine grows.

♀ Scottish Crossbill hanging 'parrot fashion' from the branch of a 'bog' pine on a nest material gathering foray.

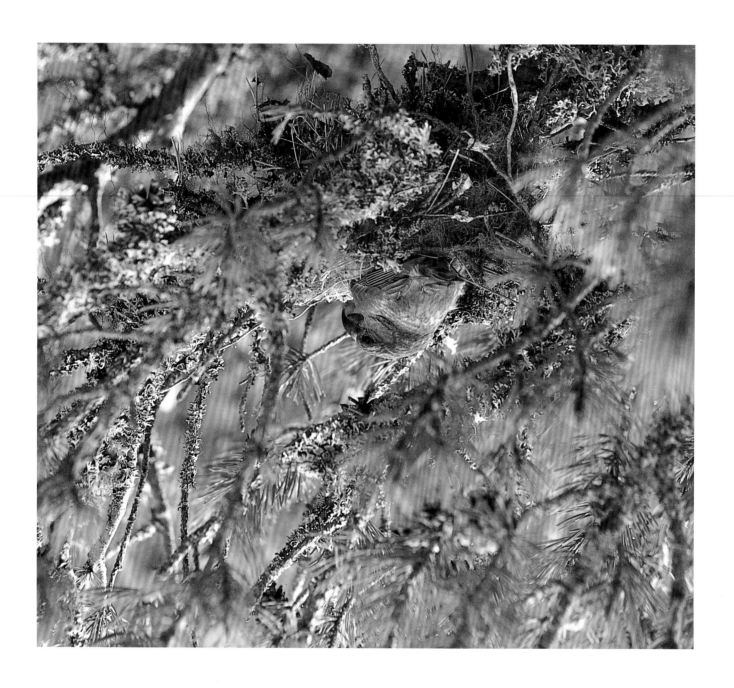

The female crossbill brooded her young, hidden in a branch 30 feet above the forest floor.

manner perfectly described by the late Desmond Nethersole-Thompson, doyen of ornithologists and author of the classic book *Pine Crossbills.*

'In late winter and early spring there is never a dull moment when the crossbills are pairing up in their flocks. One, two or three cocks then sometimes court a particular hen by "low intensity courtship feeding". The cock now sometimes seizes the hen's beak and the two birds sway rhythmically together with their beaks interlocked.

Singing loudly, a cock also often describes an arc between two trees. By exaggerating his wing beats and spreading and slightly depressing his tail, he displays his brilliant scarlet rump patch to the hen.

Before the groups disperse you often see two pairs threatening one another, the cocks and hens crouching and scolding angrily. Cocks now threaten cocks, and hens usually menace other hens. Threatening often leads to fighting, when the two scarlet birds, singing stridently, grapple claw-to-claw. Occasionally two cocks drop to the ground where they still fight and screech.'

We saw nothing so dramatic, but, being keen to locate a nest, followed the pair all morning, until losing them while re-negotiating the river. We returned to the area for several days, but failed to find them again - a typical example of crossbill elusiveness. So we diligently read Nethersole-Thompson's book for the clues that would lead us to a crossbill's nest and searched the Speyside woods with increasingly stiff necks - stiff because the nests are usually well-hidden in pine needles and lichen at the ends of branches, often 30 to 50 feet up. Sometimes, though, they nest in bog pines whose growth has been stunted by water and where even century-old trees might be only 10 to 15 feet high. As we had to build a scaffold to film the intimate details of the crossbill's breeding, a nest at this height was definitely preferable.

Within days, much to our surprise and delight, we had found a nest in the top of the most insignificant of trees, only 10 feet high, but our problems were just beginning. A crow also found the nest and ate the eggs. Two more nests were lost to predators that year. Then,

the following season, after much searching, we found a pair feeding their young on an isolated limb 40 feet up. We had just finished bringing all the scaffolding to the site when we noticed a red squirrel running away from the nest. A quick check with a ladder confirmed that it had just eaten the last of the chicks.

Scientists have suggested that the crossbill's habit of nesting so early - they sometimes lay eggs in February - makes them unusually vulnerable to predation. Though the cover provided by pine needles around the nest has no seasonal variation (the Scots pine is not deciduous), predators have less to eat in late winter and less to distract them from their search for food. A forester friend of ours, David Whittaker, described how careful crossbills are to avoid detection:

'Crossbills do not normally call loudly near the nest. During building the male sings a quiet subsong above the working female. When visiting a brooding female he usually lands first at the top of a nearby tree. From there his contact calls are quite soft. The female's reply is very soft indeed. Predators might be attracted by the male's flight from his exposed perch directly to the nest where the female's begging calls may be heard. Loud "tooping" is a sign of aggression or alarm. If other crossbills invade their privacy a noisy slanging match and a certain amount of chasing ensues. Their reaction to human presence is to alarm briefly before departing the area when nest building or, later on in the breeding season, to alarm from the tree tops until they consider that the threat has moved away. Such behaviour must make nests very vulnerable to crows, which can often be observed taking their cues from man. Squirrels I would guess to be less of a threat, only finding nests casually when foraging.'

But for whatever reason, we had lost all seven nests found during the previous two years, even before we'd put a photographic hide near them, so we hoped our last year would be a good cone year, and it was. As we arrived in the spring, crossbills appeared to be everywhere. Chaffinches are usually the commonest bird in the Caledonian pine forests, but when seed is plentiful can be outnumbered locally by Scottish

*Crossbills are always fastidious in their choice of cones and
many are rejected as they move from tree to tree.*

crossbills. This appeared to be just such a year, and we soon found a female crossbill building a nest with such enthusiasm that she allowed us to erect the scaffold and assemble the camera in full view, just 12 feet away. Both male and female were the most confiding of birds but this confidence is not unusual. John Walpole-Bond describes in his book *Field Studies of Some Rarer British Birds* how, while hunting for crossbill nests and eggs in 1914, he stroked a sitting hen and 'stranger still, (she) actually perched on my fingers as I examined her treasures'. Nethersole-Thompson also describes how a hen once landed on his fingers and allowed him to hold her, and he writes with affection of the charm of her trust and the vivid recollection of the sharp resinous scent of her body.

Tame though our pair were, our success with the nest was short-lived, for they abandoned it a few days later, after they had added a few feathers to the flimsy structure. They prospected another site about 200 yards away, with the hen paying several visits to a branch end, twisting and turning in the spot she felt suitable for building while the male called excitedly nearby. But she gave up this site too, enhancing the crossbill's reputation for being very fussy about its choice of nest-site. After a further two days' frustrating search we found the pair building not far away and were at last rewarded with the privilege of being able to film the whole process of nest-construction.

The nest was situated in the uppermost limb of a bushy bog pine, only 12 feet high, and while the male sang and guarded the female and the territory from intruders, she busied herself gathering twigs for the nest. She did this in the lower branches and once again her selection was thorough, for she combed through the twigs meticulously, sometimes swinging upside down and climbing along parrot fashion, using beak and claws. Several twigs were snipped off with her secateur like bill and discarded before she decided one was suitable and flew back to the nest with it. The twig was then positioned carefully, sometimes several places being tried before she was satisfied, whereupon she shook it rapidly up and down to secure the structure. In the early days of construction she collected twigs from the nest tree itself, but she must have exhausted the supply of suitable material quickly, for she was soon searching an ever-widening area around the nest, always escorted by her mate.

Bursts of intense activity were interspersed with periods of feeding, when the male would call the female to join him and both would bound off into some undiscovered part of the forest. When they returned, he took no part in the construction but would sometimes come to the nest to inspect progress, which was rapid. Perhaps because of the previous failures, she seemed anxious to lay her eggs; within five days she had a substantial structure hidden among the pine needles and proceeded to line it with dry grass and moss. At first, these were gathered from the ground beneath the tree, but she soon became more selective, sometimes flying half a mile to a farmyard to bring back hens' feathers. Bundles of sheep wool were also added, and most interestingly I thought, she made several visits to a dead pine stump, ripping off beakfuls of dry wood pulp to line the nest. As if aware of the danger of predation, her final day's activity was spent painstakingly searching for any tell-tale bits of carelessly dropped nest-material. She pulled bits of wool off the branches, grass from the pine needles, a feather from the ground, and spent ages hanging on to the bottom of the nest to remove any straggling wool and grass from her construction. All this spare material was discarded a good distance away - after which she flew off and fed for a long time among the cones of a majestic granny pine.

At dawn the next day she laid her first pale blue-white egg and a week later she was sitting tight. Another three days passed, by which time the embryo chicks inside her four eggs would have been well on their way to becoming young crossbills. Then tragedy struck. A carrion crow spotted the male feeding the hen crossbill as she sat incubating, swooped down, drove her off the nest and ate the eggs. We never saw the pair again.

In vain, we sought another nest, searching the giant pines of Abernethy and Inshriach, combing through the scattered forest that tumbled down from the snow-covered corries of Glen Einich, walking into the vast expanse of Rothiemurchus. Overhead, skeins of geese sped northwards, driven by the wind towards their Arctic breeding grounds. Their passing was just one response to the coming of spring and, as their calls were drawn away to far-off lands, another sound, a subdued but insistent tapping, rang out from among the ancient pines.

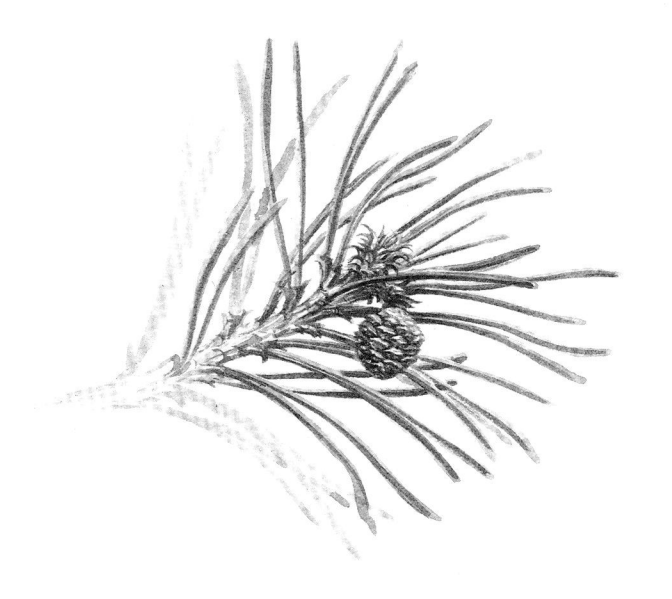

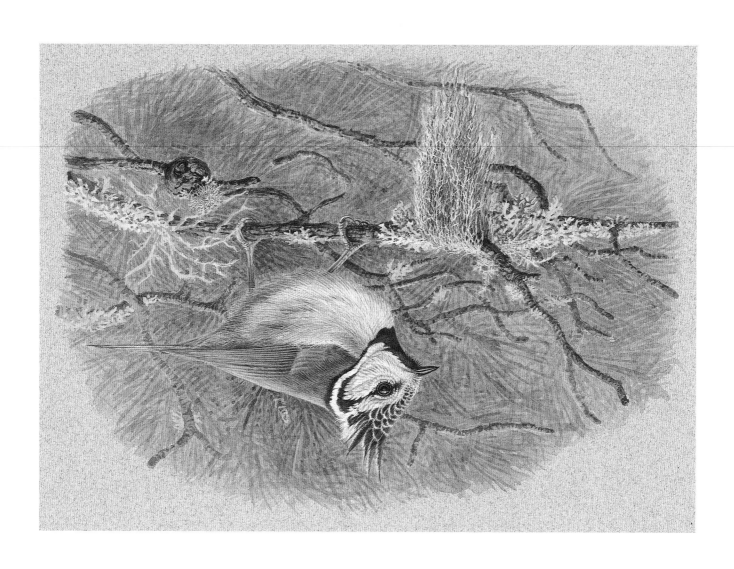

CHAPTER THREE

Great Excavations

Wind roared through the wood like the torrents of an angry river. A million needles hissed in the blast. Branches thrashed violently but did not break, and the towering trunks remained unbowed. They stood with patient, upright dignity, as they had through centuries of storms, each year reaching ever higher into wild Highland skies.

But each year takes its toll. Once in a while an ancient pine, its gnarled roots prised loose from the glacial gravels, falls crashing to the forest floor. Death for a tree, however, holds the promise of life for hordes of hungry insects. Attracted by the rotting wood, they burrow beneath the protective bark to reach the rich tinder within. There, sheltered from prying eyes and probing beaks, they breed in numbers beyond counting. Elsewhere, in less exposed parts of the forest, many trees die but remain standing, and for decades their slowly decaying flesh and bones provide shelter for other creatures of Caledon.

Searching deeper in the forest, we became aware of a faint tapping sound which seemed to be coming from a dead tree in the middle of a clearing. Stripped of its bark, its skeletal limbs were gnarled and twisted, as if it had fought a long and painful battle with death but still remained stubbornly upright, defying the slow march of time, and we circled it in admiration as we tried to pinpoint the source of the mysterious tapping. Eventually we found a small hole a few feet from the ground and waited until the tapping stopped. After a brief pause, a sliver of wood appeared, held by the beak of a small grey bird with a prominent topknot. It was a crested tit, one of the most delightful specialists of the ancient Caledonian pine forests. The tit flew off to another pine nearby, scattered the rotten wood into the wind and returned to its task of making a hole inside the tree. Few birds in the world excavate their nest sites, and the crested tit is especially unusual as it does not appear to be adapted for such a task, lacking the woodpecker's reinforced skull and chisel beak. Yet still it hacked away at the crumbling timber with tireless vigour.

As we settled down to watch, we became aware that we were not the only observers in the forest.

Nearby, sitting silently beneath a tree with a notebook and tape-recorder, was a young woman in a weather-beaten jacket and faded jeans. It was Helen Young from Dundee University, carrying out research for her doctoral thesis, the purpose of which was to find out what crested tits need to survive and prosper. Now that the Royal Society for the Protection of Birds is a major owner of this unique woodland her results will be invaluable in helping the society to manage its native pines in a way that should benefit the tits and encourage greater breeding success.

With the exception of a few bogs and mountain tops, these old forests are arguably the only native habitat in Britain which has never been modified by man. Although many relic species of the original Caledonian forest have been lost, the crested tit has clung on, confined almost exclusively to these last native pinewoods because they still provide numerous rotten stumps in which to excavate a nest.

Accurate historical records of crested tit distribution go back only 150 years, but it is assumed that they occurred throughout the Great Wood and that the destruction of the forest brought about a parallel reduction of crested tits. There are now probably fewer than 1,000 pairs, making them not only our rarest tit but also one of our rarest British birds.

In the forest of Strathspey the crested tit has always been looked upon as a special rarity. Writing from Edinburgh in 1844, a Mr T. Macpherson Grant said: 'I procured two Crested tits near Carrbridge which I now have stuffed. They are the only specimens which have ever been seen by the birdstuffers here.' And in 1847 Mr Lewis Dunbar was introduced to the celebrated naturalist John Gould, who did not believe the crested tit bred in the Highlands; so he was asked to send a nest and eggs, with the two old birds in the flesh, by post, for the princely sum of £5. Harvey-Brown describes an incident in 1892 in his historic book *The Fauna of the Moray Basin*: 'The keeper found the nest first about one o'clock and shot the two birds, a deed we deprecated, yet, as it was the only fresh nest we had ever obtained we yielded a somewhat willing assent.' He goes on to say, somewhat contradictorily:

'We have little fear of the crested tit becoming rare through man's direct agency, as the area they cover is an extensive one, and to find the nests requires considerable search.' Since then, of course, man's direct agency has indeed reduced the crested tit, by destroying most of the forest.

As we sat together under the ancient pines, watching the excavations continue, Helen described what she had discovered during her three years' research into the secret lives of these enchanting birds. Crested tits have been recorded nesting in great spotted woodpecker holes and squirrel dreys, holes in the ground (a habit they share with coal tits), old metal fence posts - even in the base of the nests of birds of prey. Nest-boxes are usually ignored, which is not surprising when they are so fussy about choosing a suitable dead tree.

Prospecting for a site normally starts in late March when the pair seem to explore every rotten stump in their territory - as many as 50 in a mature forest. They may even excavate several holes, perhaps three or four, before making a final choice. Any dead tree with a depth of three to four inches of friable wood is suitable, but trees of less than about eight inches in diameter are chosen only if the hard centre is offset. Such a tree is delightfully described as having 'eccentric heartwood'. A suitable tree must also have a hard outer parchment, and crested tits prefer trees that have grown hard branch stubs, often excavating the hole close to these to make use of the extra support and protection they provide for the nest.

Once a tree has died its demise is slow, and it may take more than 10 years for fungi to soften up the wood sufficiently for a nest-hole to be chipped out. The nest takes about three weeks to complete, and Helen derived much wry pleasure from pointing out that the female alone does all the work while the male merely stands guard nearby, offering encouragement

Normally, crested tits start to prospect for a nest site in late March, when the pair seem to explore every rotten stump in their territory.

GREAT EXCAVATIONS

*Such a dead tree is delightfully described as
having 'eccentric heartwood'.*

*Hatching takes place in mid to late May and at
first both parents feed the brood.*

by trilling an excited song. The nest is lined at the end
of April - a process which takes five to six days - with
moss as the main material, though roe deer hair and
feathers are sometimes used.

At the end of the season Helen strips out these
nests to inspect them for insects and parasites. Each
nest yields an extraordinary amount of material - at
least two fistfuls, and alive with fleas. She once stored a
crested tit's nest through the winter in a plastic bag. In
the warmth of the mossy nest lining the fleas thrived
and multiplied. By next spring there were thousands of
them - no doubt the reason why nest sites are seldom
used a second time!

The five or six diminutive white eggs, decorated
with red spots, are laid in early May. It is the smallest
clutch of all the tit species and no one knows why.
Like most school reports, Helen suggests they 'could
do better'. During incubation, the female sits for 40
minutes, then leaves to be fed by the male in a nearby

tree. He also feeds her on the nest when she is
incubating or brooding small young.

Hatching takes place in mid to late May. At first
both parents feed the brood but a point is reached
where one or the other takes sole responsibility - it can
be the male or the female - and the other adult
disappears. Helen could not discover whether it then
defends the territory or stores food in readiness for the
winter; but when the brood fledge in early June the
second parent sometimes reappears. This was certainly
the case with one of Helen's study nests which we
observed closely, from both outside the tree trunk
and inside.

Over several days we had carefully moved our
hide closer to the nest until it was right up against the
tree. From there we were able to chisel away at the
rotten trunk without being seen until we had a small
observation port through which we could watch the
young being fed. The fibre-optic lights we had

38

squeezed behind the flaky bark revealed a secret world of wooden stalactites and gnarled branch roots festooned with cobwebs. Huddled at the base of this fibrous grotto, surrounded by moss and sheep's wool, were the chicks, six fluffy balls each adorned with a miniature punkish crest.

The chicks lay silent until a distant trill in the woods announced the approach of the female, whereupon six beaks gaped wide open and six tiny bodies shook excitedly in anticipation. There came a faint scratch of claws on a branch outside and the female appeared, straddling the nest as she thrust small caterpillars and spiders into the urgently begging mouths. Supply seldom seemed to satisfy demand, but they quickly settled down again while she waited for a chick to defecate upwards and then flew off with the faecal sac to deposit it a safe distance from the nest, so as not to alert predators - a wise precaution. During our two years in the forest we recorded three instances of nests being ripped out by squirrels or pine martens, and Helen's research indicates that 17% of all nests are lost to predation. So the chicks' silence is imperative while the parents are away foraging for food in the trees.

Crested tits find most of their prey among the needles and flaky bark of the Scots pine, and their foraging follows a regular pattern each year. During April they feed high in the canopy, extracting seeds from the cones as they ripen and split. This period lasts only two to three weeks and they spend the rest of the year searching for insects, usually high in the canopy but also in the forest understorey of heather, juniper and blackberry. One food item is particularly important. This is the caterpillar of a moth the foresters call the 'pine-looper', which becomes particularly numerous in the autumn, sometimes reaching pest proportions.

With each passing day the feeding of the chicks became even more frenetic. By the end of May the

The female tempted the chicks to fly by offering them food, which was then snatched out of their mouths as they teetered on the lip of the nest hole.

female, having been left to raise the brood on her own, was flitting to the nest every few minutes with a fresh beakful of caterpillars, spiders and even a few wood ants. But the climax came in early June. After each feed, the chicks fluttered their stubby wings in preparation for their first flight into the unknown world outside, and the more precocious youngsters now climbed up the inside of the nest and appeared at the entrance, where they begged noisily for food and looked out into the forest. Their first views of their future home seemed to be greeted with a mixture of curiosity and fear, and the female, sensing their hesitation, tempted them to fly by offering food but snatching it out of their mouths before their beaks could snap shut. Driven almost demented, they teetered on the lip of the nest-hole. Then, one by one, they launched out on their maiden voyage, whirring into nearby trees with surprising success for a first flight.

Within minutes the entire brood had fledged and the female gathered them together and led them into the densest pine branches of the forest canopy, where she hoped they might be hidden from the prying eye of marauding sparrowhawks. Perched safely, each youngster preened itself, snuggled its head under a fluffy wing and went to sleep. The nest-tree, having been the centre of so much noise and activity, now stood deserted in the forest clearing, continuing its silent process of decay.

Next day, the young tits dispersed into two groups and were soon following the female on foraging trips through the upper branches. They moved with quick, hurried movements, as if they knew their lives were too fleeting to waste a single second. A fledgling's life expectancy is painfully short, just one to two years, with only a very few surviving to greet a third Highland spring. By the following April, when wild goose skeins wing north over the trees and their yelping voices drift down into the darkest shadows of the wood, only one in three adult crested tits would still be alive, and most of their offspring would have perished in the deep frosts that fill the Highland glens. But the survivors would know again the warmth of the returning sun.

As days grew longer and burns brimmed with meltwater from the high hills, they would hear the silence of the winter wood broken by the song of a thousand birds, and add their own excited trilling. Once more the muffled tapping would begin inside the dead pines. And as we sat and listened we became aware of another sound, like fine rain falling on the forest floor. It was the feet of a million wood ants venturing forth in search of food. Spring had returned.

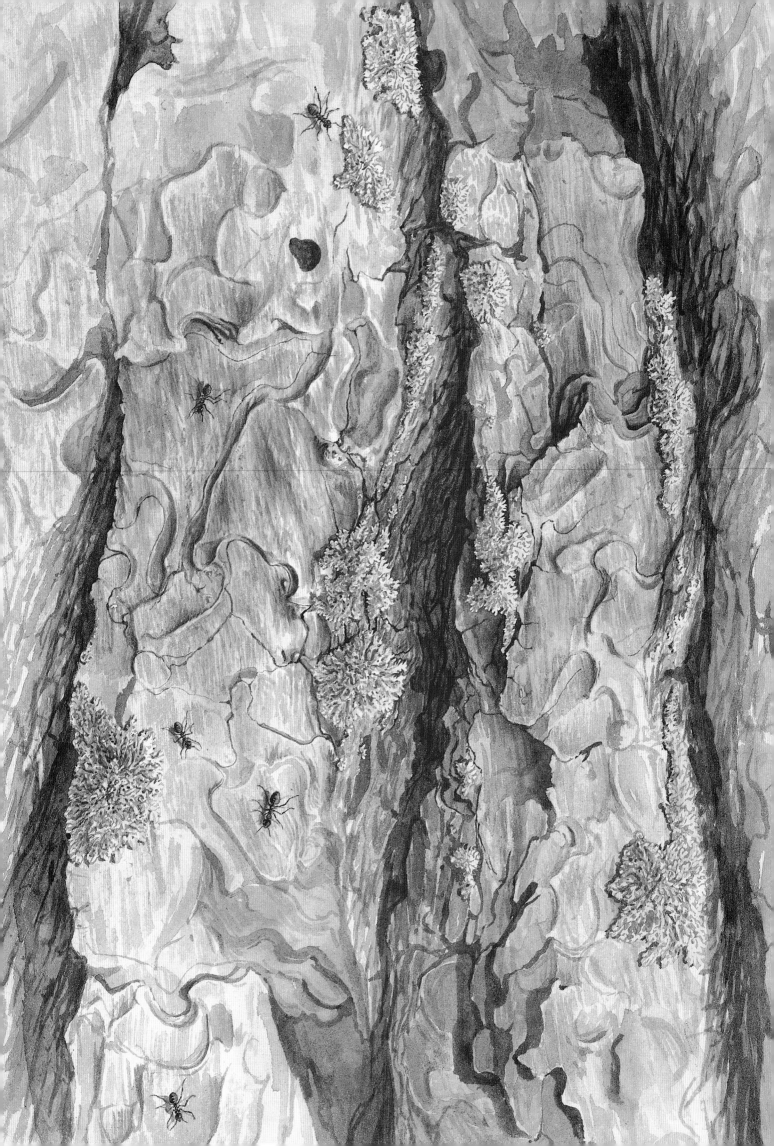

CHAPTER FOUR
The Mound Builders

The hills of Speyside shone hoary white with an overnight dusting of snow, but in the woods of Abernethy where the crossbills were feeding, there was no doubt that spring had arrived. Already, cock chaffinches with pink chests shouted their territorial songs from the treetops, and willow warblers, newly arrived from their wintering grounds in the Sahel, filled the woods with sibilant whisperings. A tree creeper worked its way like a feathered mouse down the fissured trunk of a granny pine, probing for spiders under the peeling bark. Somewhere in the distance a great spotted woodpecker drummed on a dead tree.

As the crossbills fed, expertly scissoring open the pine cones to get at the seeds within, they let fall a constant scatter of discarded scales. Some landed on a curious mound, a distinctive dome of dead pine needles and other forest litter which stood about three feet high among the fallen branches and straggling tufts of heather beneath the tree. Such mounds are a common feature in the woods of Abernethy. They are the rooftops of a hidden world, raised by the most numerous of all the inhabitants of the Caledonian pine forest.

Long before the Romans came to Britain the tireless legions of *Formica aquilonia* were colonizing the pinewoods of Caledon. They are the wood ants, the mound-builders of the forest floor. There are more than 40 species of ants in Britain, but the large, long-legged wood ants are by far the most impressive. In England *Formica rufa* is the most widespread, but it does not occur in Scotland. There, its place is taken by two other species, and by *Formica aquilonia*. But whereas the former are often found in open country beyond the woodlands, *Formica aquilonia* is a true insect denizen of the relic pine forests.

The wood ants belong to an ancient race of insects which evolved more than 70 million years ago. Like all insects, they have a hard external covering divided into three parts: head, thorax and abdomen. They have compound eyes but, compared to the birds and mammals of the pinewoods, their sight is limited. In the myopic world of the wood ant they are unable to detect movement more than four inches away. Instead, their world is of subtle scents and chemical signals, insect sounds and delicate vibrations, received and interpreted through their antennae. They are also equipped with powerful mandibles, and their abdomens contain poison glands of formic acid which can be squirted with great accuracy over a distance of a couple of inches.

Above the nest the crossbills were still feeding, and, as the flakes of discarded cone hit the mound, small flurries of worker ants advanced to investigate the disturbance. The workers were not yet truly active, although some were already busily repairing the domed roof of the mound. They had spent the winter in hibernation, deep in the ground beneath the great heap of pine needles whose sloping sides shrugged off the rain and snow as efficiently as any thatched cottage roof. Now, as the spring days grew longer, the sun rose higher over the forest and its slanting beams struck the nest with greater warmth, drawing both workers and queens to the surface to bask on the south-facing side of the mound. It seemed that the ants needed the sun's warmth to shake off the lethargy of their long winter sleep, and it would take several more such days before the workers would set out once again in their endless scurrying columns to forage for food in the woods.

There are many such mounds in the pine forest, and each one conceals a teeming citadel excavated by armies of industrious worker ants who use their mandibles like miniature bulldozers to bite into the soil, which is then raked into piles with the front legs, to be removed, grain by painstaking grain, and dumped on the woodland floor. The finished result is a miracle of construction: a complex maze of galleries, domed chambers and underground passageways that echo to the constant rustle and movement - faint as a whisper - of the multitude seething within.

In their building skills, the ants of the Caledonian pinewoods are no different from the diminutive yellow field ants whose grass-grown hillocks disrupt the turf of old meadows and unploughed downs in southern Britain. But, unlike the field ants, the wood ants hide their nests beneath a protective haystack of dead pine needles and other leaf litter, which serves both as a

The wood ants are the hunter-gatherers of the insect world, roaming the forest in hungry armies in a constant search for food.

roof against the rain and an ingenious south-facing solarium or night storage heater, retaining the sun's energy after dark and creating a micro-climate several degrees warmer than the air outside. Only in winter, when there is no sun to warm the nest, does the temperature drop; and even then, the roof's insulating power helps to conserve the collective body heat given off by the hibernating colony.

In this way, secure in the moist darkness of their subterranean ghettos, the wood ants live and multiply, expanding their mounds to accommodate their growing broods. The mounds may last for years. Some may have been occupied for decades, and a single colony may contain more than half a million ants.

Wood ants appear to be particularly sensitive to air temperatures, and the fickle Scottish weather therefore plays an important part in their lives. Strong winds, rain and even bright sunlight tend to slow down their activity; while a very cold snap or a spell of

heavy rain is enough to stop them foraging altogether. On the other hand, should the temperature rise by 10 degrees or so during the morning, providing the sultry Highland summer days they most enjoy, they respond by moving around with redoubled energy.

Emerging in the mornings, the workers circle the mound and then set out in long columns along the half-dozen or so regular highways radiating from the nest. Wood ants are skilled climbers, and hunt for their prey both in the trees and on the ground. Their victims are numerous, and include house flies, crane flies, midges - even other ants - and the caterpillars of sawflies and moths, such as the pine beauty, whose larvae defoliate the woods. In this respect the ants can be seen as valuable allies for the forester, protecting his woodlands from a host of insect pests as well as recycling the litter of the forest floor.

All day long the ant highways are alive with movement. Every day, each worker brings back to the

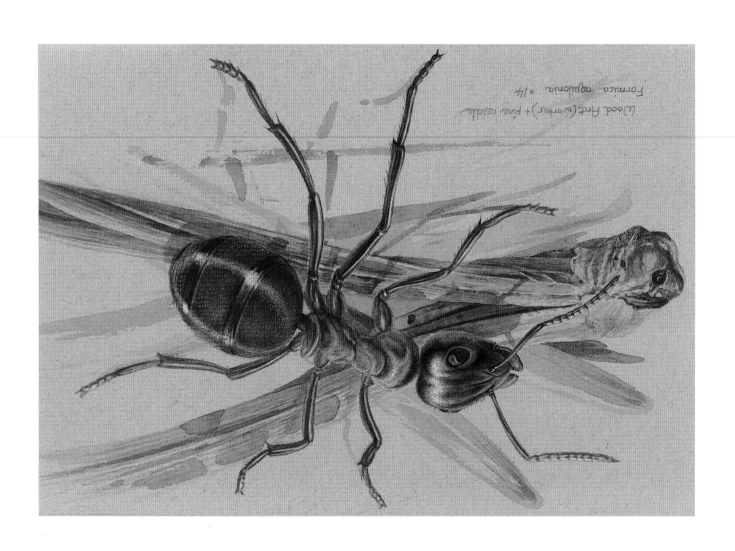

Wood Ant (worker) + pine needle
Formica aquilonia ×14

nest roughly one and a half times its own weight in food, and the entire workforce of a big colony may collect as many as 100,000 insects each day. The area over which the colony regularly forages could be described as its home range, and includes whole trees, connected by regular trackways to form a single realm - vigorously defended against intruders from other colonies - with the nest at its heart. Often the most used tracks are those leading to pines infested with aphids - minute, sap-sucking insects which live among the twigs and produce a sweet secretion known as honeydew. For the ants this is a favourite food source, lacking in protein but immensely rich in sugars, acids, alcohols, salts and vitamins. Once the wood ants have located an aphid colony, they tend them like cows, removing other insect enemies and 'milking' the aphids by stroking them until they release the precious droplets of honeydew. Over a quarter of a ton of sugar solution is carried to a single nest each season.

In spite of this benign relationship, wood ants are essentially predators. They are the hunter-gatherers of the insect world, roaming the forest in hungry armies in a constant search for food. Their prey is detected by vibration and by scent. Once it is in view, some four inches away, the hunting ants advance with sinister stealth, heads forward, jaws agape and antennae laid back. Then suddenly they pounce, running forward to grip the victim with their pincer-like mandibles, and bringing round the gaster - the bulbous terminal section of their bodies - to deliver a lethal squirt of formic acid. If, as sometimes happens, the prey is larger than themselves, it is simply overwhelmed by weight of numbers and hauled laboriously back to the nest.

It is such acts of co-operation which have made ants so successful, occupying the earth in their untold millions. Their well-ordered society, with its rigid hierarchies of queens and workers, could be said to be the world's oldest civilization. How they rally to a common purpose is still not fully understood; but they appear to communicate by a mysterious language of chemical signals which can warn of danger, summon workers for urgent repairs if the nest is damaged, or convey the whereabouts of a new food source.

The secret world of the wood ant is full of such mysteries. How, for instance, do they foretell the coming of winter? All British ants hibernate, workers and queens alike, and the wood ants of the Caledonian forest are no exception. As early as August a curious lassitude seems to permeate the entire colony. The larvae in the nest slow down their rate of growth and begin laying up stores of food in their reserve tissues. At the same time the queens begin to reduce their egg-laying until eventually they cease altogether. As for the workers, they become increasingly lethargic and no longer leave the nest to forage.

The weeks pass. The heather flares purple on the hills and the blaeberries ripen in the woods. By the time the Highland birches have begun to glow smoky gold in the shortening days, the great mass of ants will have retreated deep into the ground once more, there to remain in a state of hibernation until spring. Then, as the sun's returning warmth penetrates the nest, it awakens the workers, who break out again into the light to resume their life of toil. The queens, too, stir from their winter sleep. Deep in their royal chambers they begin again to produce the eggs that will become the next generation in the long dynasty of the mound-builders.

The queens were fertilized after the nuptial flights of a previous midsummer when, for one brief moment of freedom, they took wing and rose above the pinewoods into the golden warmth of a long Highland evening. But on returning to earth they broke off their wings - a symbolic act which would bind them for ever after to the underworld. Drawn to the waiting queens by powerful chemical lures, the males become willing victims of the wood ants' macabre mating ritual. Even while still joined in the throes of copulation, the queens round on the hapless males and cut off their abdomens - but not before they have received enough sperm to last a lifetime. Then they crawl away to spend the rest of their days below ground.

The smooth white eggs are looked after by the workers, who constantly fuss over them, turning and licking them clean of fungi and mites. In time they hatch to become hairless grubs, which lie helplessly in the nurseries, sucking juices offered by the workers, who mix liquids extracted from chewed-up insect prey with honeydew and their own saliva. Fattened and cosseted, the grubs grow quickly, bursting out of their

skins several times until, after a period of pupation, they emerge as adult ants.

The wood ants are not the only insects associated with these northern forests. In all, more than 90 different species occur in the pinewoods. Among them are the pine weevil, which strips the soft skin from young pine shoots, the black pine beetle, which attacks the roots of the tree, and the timberman, a handsome longhorn beetle found only in Scotland, whose larvae burrow into the decaying wood.

Some insects actually depend on the presence of the wood ants to complete their own life cycle. One species of chafer beetle lays its eggs in the roof of the wood ants' nest, which becomes food for the larvae when they hatch. The larvae themselves are protected against the unwelcome attention of the ants by a tough, bristly skin and the ability to burrow swiftly to safety if attacked. When fully grown, the chafer grubs spin a cocoon from which, in time, the adult beetle will emerge.

Even more bizarre is the cuckoo-like behaviour of the clytra beetle, whose larvae feed on wood ant pellets. The beetle lays its eggs enclosed in capsules made of its own droppings. These eggs are picked up by the worker ants and taken into the mound, perhaps because they look like suitable nest-building material but more probably, scientists now believe, because the eggs give off a chemical pheromone which the wood ants find irresistible. There, once they have hatched,

the clytra larvae grow rapidly on the ants' eggs, building progressively bigger and better protective shells of soil, droppings and leaf litter which enable them to live unmolested inside the mound. Eventually, to complete the cycle, they emerge from the wood ants' nest as adult beetles.

Sometimes, however, the methodical lives of the mound-builders are disturbed by much larger intruders. In Glen Tanar, the wood ants emerging from their nest at the beginning of April were unaware of the huge, turkey-like bird approaching through the trees. Its plumage was the colour of old beech leaves, the upper parts beautifully barred and flecked with black, so that its body seemed netted with shadows except where the early morning sun struck rich coppery glints from its lustrous breast feathers. It was a hen capercaillie, the giant grouse of the Caledonian forest. Capercaillies will sometimes seek out the dry mound of a wood ant nest for dust-bathing - with disastrous results for its inhabitants. But on this occasion the nest was spared.

As the hen drew closer, an unearthly sound rang out from somewhere deeper in the forest. At once she stopped in her tracks, tilting her head this way and that to listen, until the noise died away as mysteriously as it had begun, leaving the glen locked in a single silence. Then it began again, louder and this time unmistakable: the wheezing, popping, knife-grinding cry of a cock capercaillie displaying in the dawn.

CHAPTER FIVE

Sitting Tight

Every year during the third week of April, the ancient pines of Glen Tanar echo to the extraordinary calls of the cock capercaillie as their springtime ritual reaches its peak. In some years their bizarre posturings begin as early as January. Often they will still be calling and displaying well into May. Indeed, displays can be seen throughout the summer, but April is invariably the peak time to see and hear the giant grouse of Caledon.

A cock caper is one of the most spectacular sights the Highland pine forests can offer. With metallic green breast and vermilion wattles, like blobs of hot sealing wax above each beady eye, he is an impressive creature, about 10 pounds in weight, almost the size of an eagle.

On rare occasions at this time of year, a cock capercaillie can be aggressive enough to threaten even human intruders. Just such a bird existed in Inshriach Forest during 1988, a magnificent male we christened Angus, after a friend of ours. He became a notorious character, rushing out of the forest to challenge passing walkers or mountain bikers. One April day we were admiring his courage as he blustered at us on a heathery bank - an eyeball to eyeball confrontation from only two feet away. Suddenly he looked up and at once his feathers subsided, all passion deflated, and he crept back into the dense cover of the forest. We stared into the sky to see what had frightened him. At first we could see nothing; but then we scanned the clouds with binoculars and immediately picked up two dark specks - a pair of golden eagles circling high above the glen. It was an impressive demonstration of just how sharp-sighted the capercaillie must be - and how hard it must be for an eagle to catch them napping.

Another much-loved caper was living in the forests of Glen Tanar during the 1970s. He was christened Henry by our friend Jimmy Oswald, the estate's head keeper, and anyone trespassing on Henry's territory during April would be attacked. For many years he was the dominant male on the famous leks, or displaying grounds, of Glen Tanar, until one day he overstepped the mark and attacked a young forester who had never encountered an aggressive caper before. The young lad was so frightened he turned on Henry and killed him with a stick.

Watch a cock caper on his lek, and you will see what a formidable sight he can be. Slowly he advances on his feathered feet, puffed up with lust, his black turkey tail fanned out, neck erect and nose in the air like some apoplectic old dowager. Then from somewhere deep down in that black and swollen throat a guttural hiccup emerges, a bubble of sound that breaks from his upraised ivory bill as a puff of steam and drifts away in the chill morning air. His grotesque serenade is about to begin.

The dawn light catches his glossy wings. The hiccups grow louder, like the clatter of hooves. No wonder the Highland Gaels called him *capull-choille* - the horse of the woods. Suddenly there comes a champagne-cork 'pop', and his repertoire climaxes with a series of wheezes and knife-sharpening rasps, leaving the forest stunned and silent.

His entire performance - the calling, the strutting, his sudden three-foot leaps into the air - has the desired effect. Soon he is the centre of an admiring audience of hens; though other cock birds also gather to contest the right to mate. Some display grounds may attract half a dozen cocks. In 1961 Roy Dennis, the RSPB's Highlands officer, watched fifteen males competing in front of twenty hens at a lek in Abernethy Forest, but that was exceptional.

Round and round the challengers go, circling each other like Sumo wrestlers. Everything about this ritualized display of aggression would appear to be designed to avoid direct conflict; in the natural world, intimidation is always preferable to physical violence and the risk of injury. Yet cock capers fight often, and when they do - coming together in a vicious explosion of buffeting wings and snapping bills - the pair may not cease until one of them is left for dead.

The victor, beard bristling like an angry raven, looks around for other contenders. They will bide their time and maybe try to mate with the hens while he is busy fighting. But for the moment he is the undisputed master of the lek, the lord of the ring, treading the hens which offer themselves for mating with arched backs and drooping wings.

The ancient pines of Glen Tanar echo to the extraordinary calls of the cock capercaillie and he is soon the centre of an admiring audience of hens.

The eggs are laid on the ground, usually in a hollow under a tree, and are covered with dead pine needles and bits of heather until - after two weeks - the clutch is complete. Then, relying on her camouflage as the best defence against detection, the speckled hen sits so tight that it is possible to walk within a foot or two of her motionless form and still not flush her.

Within a month the chicks emerge and grow quickly. This is the most vulnerable time in their lives, when they are at risk from every predator in the woods. No doubt this is why, long before they are fully grown, they are able to flutter short distances over the heather.

During these first few weeks the chicks feed mostly on insects. Later they will find heather shoots, bilberries and rowan berries; and when January comes they begin to rely heavily on pine shoots, whose resinous tang impregnates their flesh. Foresters hated the capercaillie for its damaging habit of shearing off

the tender tips and leader buds, stunting their precious trees, and must have shed few tears when the original Highland stock died out in the late 18th-century. By then, felling of the woods had so restricted their range that the few dwindling survivors were soon hunted to extinction - the last two native Scottish capers being shot for a wedding feast at Balmoral.

Fifty years passed in which the relic pines of Caledon no longer rang to the clip-clop voice of the horse of the woods. In 1827 the Earl of Fife attempted to reintroduce the species at Mar Lodge in Aberdeenshire, but without success. Then, 10 years later, Lord Breadalbane brought 13 cocks and 19 hens from Sweden and turned them loose in the woods at Taymouth Castle. Within 25 years there were more than 1,000 birds on the estate, and in 1894 others were returned to Strathnairn, near Inverness. From these secure bridgeheads the birds spread out and consolidated in their old Caledonian stamping

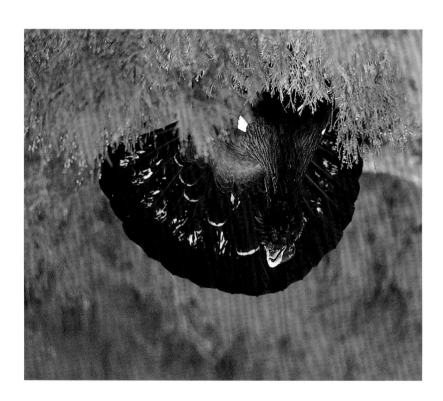

April is invariably the time to see and hear the giant grouse of Caledon.

grounds. It seemed that the giant grouse of the pinewoods had come home to stay. However, having peaked in the 1950s, their numbers have again become much reduced over the last two decades, giving cause for concern. Cold, wet weather during the period of the hatch has been blamed, but scientists are attempting to discover all the reasons for the decline and propose solutions to the problem.

Certainly the woods in springtime would seem strangely silent and empty without the calls of the cock capercaillies. In these sharp Highland mornings, when snow still gleams from the high corries, all sound carries farther on the cold air, and it was now that we began to hear the dove-like bubbling of the blackcocks, perhaps the most evocative sound of the Caledonian spring.

Black grouse are birds of the forest fringes. Larger than the red grouse but only half the size of the capercaillie, they frequent the upper limits of the woods,

browsing on birch buds and pine shoots. Where the trees give way to open hillsides they also feed on choice shoots of young heather, supplemented in autumn by the moorland fruits of bilberry and crowberry.

Like the capercaillie, the blackcocks, as male black grouse are known, also gather for the strange courtship rituals of the lek. (The word comes from the Gaelic *lace* - a level place - and refers to the open arena in the heather where the birds conduct their formal dances.) Many leks are traditional, the same patch of open ground being used for generations. Here, resplendent in their glossy blue-black breeding plumage, with their startling red eyebrows and lyre-shaped tails, the males take up their positions within the lek and defend them against all comers. Sometimes well over a score of males may be present, with the dominant blackcock usually to be found commanding the centre of the ring, and their eerie twirling calls soon attracting small groups of females - known as greyhens.

Hens gather in the trees before dropping to the
ground to offer themselves for mating.

Blackcocks also gather for the strange courtship rituals of the lek but
they remain vulnerable to keen-eyed golden eagles.

When the first greyhen approaches, the cocks immediately display to her, showing off their dazzling white under-tail feathers or bowing with wings outstretched and bodies pressed to the ground as if imploring her to mate with them.

When mating is over the greyhens disperse and fly off to the open moorland, gliding on downcurved pinions to drop into the heather where the nest - a simple scrape on the ground - will eventually accommodate up to 10 freckled eggs. As with the capercaillie, the young can fly long before they are fully grown, but even as adults they will remain vulnerable to the hunters of the skies - the keen-eyed peregrines and marauding eagles.

All winter long the eagles had sailed out over the great, sad hills in their endless quest for carrion. The Arctic nights and howling blizzards take a heavy toll among the wandering herds of red deer. Cold wet springs are even greater killers of deer, and many a

proud stag, his best years over, will not see another Highland summer. In time his bones will be sucked into the peat to nourish the heather and the bog asphodel, but the eagles will eat his flesh.

The harder the weather, the greater the number of corpses in the hills and the better the eagles fare, for the huge birds seem impervious to the cold. Sometimes we would even see them flying in the teeth of an advancing snowstorm, with their dark wings crooked against the blast.

Now spring had come, like an unstoppable tide, rising through the glens on a mist of new leaves. Already, tight green croziers of bracken were thrusting through the old year's litter to unfurl in the sun's increasing warmth. Cuckoos called among the birches, and the eagles had long since forsaken their carrion diet to hunt grouse and hares in the hills, black game and red squirrels in the pinewoods. We had been watching one particular pair of eagles since the

c55 days old

eagle chick ~20 days old
+ unhatched egg

granny pine.

These birds were one of more than 400 pairs which make the Scottish breeding population of golden eagles one of the most important in Europe. The male was known to be at least a dozen years old, the female slightly younger, and their history in this valley is typical of the changing fortunes all eagles have faced over the past 100 years.

Eagles have been known to live in the vicinity at least since 1870, when they nested among the high crags at the head of the valley. They have bred regularly but not always successfully. During the Great War, in the spring of 1915, the nest was robbed and its two eggs taken; but the pair were back the following year. Golden eagles are conservative birds. Not only do they mate for life but they remain faithful to the same eyries year after year. Some sites have been occupied by generations of eagles - even though alternative eyries within the home range are also used from time to time; so it was with the birds of this glen. In 1945 and 1946 they bred successfully, raising one youngster each year. For a while, in the 1950s, they failed to breed. Maybe a new pair were taking over; but in 1958 two young were raised.

In the spring of 1961 the nest was robbed. It was robbed again the following year, and the egg thieves left their footprints in the snow beneath the crag. Nevertheless the eagles continued to use their cliff site until the early 1970s, by which time increasing disturbance from tourists and hill-walkers finally drove them to seek sanctuary in the pine forest below. There, in 1975, they built a nest in an old tree, but they never used it. For the next five years no more nests were found, although a pair of eagles were seen flying with one young bird in the summer of 1980.

By 1983 a new pair had taken over the territory and raised two young. Yet even here, in the depths of the forest, their troubles were not over. In 1984 and 1985 the birds were disturbed by forest felling; and in 1988, as increasing tourist pressure brought growing numbers of visitors into their territory, the birds were again disturbed at a critical time and failed to breed.

In desperation, conservationists built a nest out of pine branches in a tree in the loneliest and least frequented part of the forest where the eagles would not be harassed; and in 1989 they adopted it, to everybody's amazement and delight - amazement because the golden eagle is so often reluctant to forsake its old familiar eyries. They soon enlarged the man-made stick pile and celebrated the move to their new residence by producing two healthy chicks. It was to this eyrie in the giant granny pine that we now regularly made our way each day to observe the birds from a hide secreted in a tree some 90 feet away.

An eagle dominates the land in which it lives like no other bird. In eagle country we constantly found ourselves sweeping the skyline, scanning likely cliffs and crags, longing for that powerful shape to launch itself out over the valley. Even when it was almost out of sight, dwindling to a dark star among the clouds, a sense of being watched still lingered.

How much stronger, then, is the immediate presence of this majestic hunter. Being close to an eagle's nest always brings a surge of excitement. Eagles are so large and so powerful, and yet so wary. Often, while we were peering at the brooding female from the darkness of the hide, she would turn her proud head, gold eyes glittering, and rake us with an implacable stare that seemed to penetrate the very soul. Then it would seem that she must have seen us; and yet she would not leave. Instead, shuffling the dark mantle of soft shoulder feathers which fell around her like a cloak, she would shift her position, sink deeper into the hollow comfort of the nest and continue to sit tight on the eggs which soon, we hoped, would surely hatch.

From time to time the male appeared, sometimes carrying a freshly broken pine branch which he would leave as if it were a gift to decorate the eyrie. Often we would be unaware of his presence until the female's keening voice alerted us to the fact that she had seen him drifting somewhere high overhead. Moments later he would arrive with a sudden rush of air, braking to land at the edge of the nest with heavy flaps of his broad wings, like an umbrella being shaken dry, to relieve the female's long vigil.

The days passed. The weather grew colder and the showers turned to hail in the northerly airstream, rattling through the trees and bouncing off the top of the hide, which remained snug and dry inside. By the time blue skies returned there was a chick in the nest.

The second egg never hatched, but the single nestling thrived as a result of the undivided attention it now received from its parents. In mid-morning the male arrived. We knew he was around somewhere from the behaviour of his mate, who was staring up into the sky, her head swivelling as if she was following his movements. Almost at once there was a tremendous whoosh as he came right over the hide, swooped low over the ground and then rose sharply to alight beside his mate.

A red squirrel was held in his bunched talons. Its head hung limp, revealing the bib of pale creamy fur beneath its chin. He stayed for barely a minute, then rose up once more over the trees, flapping heavily until he caught the wind and soared away out of sight.

The female, meanwhile, began to feed the chick, opening up the dead squirrel with her hooked bill and offering small gobbets of flesh to the ravenous youngster with surprising tenderness. When at last the chick was full, it shuffled deeper into the nest and closed its eyes. The female, too, rearranged herself more comfortably, tugged at a shoulder feather or two, then laid her head over her back and slept.

The sun shone. The wind sighed in the tops of the pines. Except for the territorial songs of cock chaffinches and the thin, needling cries of foraging tits, the glen and the forest together were as quiet as a church. Sometimes the breeze carried the faint calls of grouse and curlew from the distant moors, but nothing disturbed the sleeping eagle.

It was gone noon before the male returned, this time not with food but with a birch branch to adorn the nest. He stayed for an hour, preening and resting until, driven perhaps by the chick's hungry cries, he was airborne once more, rising and circling, tilting and turning on the warm thermals of air. Then, 1,000 feet above the forest, he began to slide away over the valley to where the bright gleam of water lay silver in the afternoon sun.

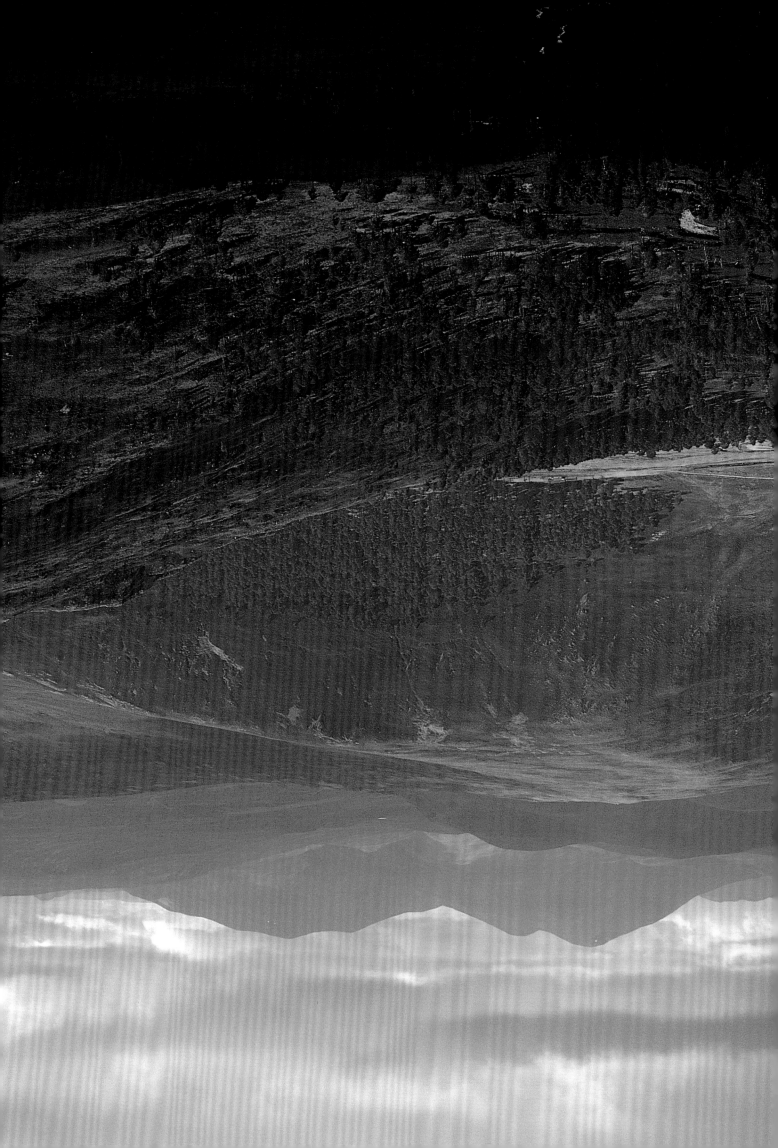

CHAPTER SIX

The Water Hunters

The eagle rose effortlessly to the high hills where the forests are scattered by the icy blast of winter. At 1,700 feet the pines have a precarious hold on life, as evidenced by their tortured frames. Some had given up the struggle to grow upright and lay prone, as if acknowledging the superiority of wind and weather. Tenuous though their existence may be, however, some of these stunted veterans have clung to the mountain crags for more than 300 years.

From his lofty rise the eagle looked down on the dark spreading forest and the silver gleam of lochans among the trees. To the west the grey bulk of the Monadhliath mountains rose to the clouds and he keeled away towards them, contracting his flight feathers to set course across the glen in a long glide.

The watchful eyes of a female osprey saw him first, and her neck stretched and stiffened. Anxiously, she mantled over her week-old chicks, calling in vain to her mate, who was hunting for trout and pike in a lochan far from the eyrie. She sprang off the nest and, with deep strokes of her brown and white wings, climbed swiftly above the unwelcome intruder, then dived at him with dramatic velocity. The unsuspecting eagle was almost raked across the back by her outstretched talons, but the whoosh of her stoop alerted him and with a flick of a wing he rolled aside. Shooting past him, it was now the osprey's turn to be disadvantaged, forcing her to twist and check as he tried to slash her with his own formidable talons. The skirmish continued, with amazing agility for such large birds, until the dogfight carried them beyond the farthest shore of the loch. Then, honour satisfied, the eagle continued its leisurely flight westward while the osprey shook her feathers and returned to her nest.

Every spring for five years the osprey and her mate had returned to their bulky structure of sticks in the top of an island pine; they are one of more than 50 pairs now nesting in the Highlands. After an absence from Scotland of nearly half a century, the first ospreys returned to breed there in 1954, and ever since those exciting early days at Loch Garten, the RSPB has guarded the colonists, keeping watch night and day to deter egg thieves. Protection has paid off, and the resulting increase in the number of Scottish ospreys has been one of the great conservation success stories of modern times.

Roy Dennis, the Society's Highlands officer, has been the man most responsible for the ospreys' recovery, locating new nests, seeking support from landowners, recording each breeding success and marking the chicks with numbered rings so that their progress can be carefully monitored. From our scaffold hide just 50 feet from the nest we could read the rings through binoculars, and we learned from Roy that this particular female had hatched in a nest near Inverness in 1981, and that her mate had fledged from the famous Loch Garten nest in 1983. Altogether, more than 500 such birds have been raised in Scotland during the last 30 years.

The male's favourite fishing spot was a marshy lochan which nestled among the ancient pines. The lochan was full of trout, eels and an abundance of pike. These predatory fish love to bask in the sunny shallows - a habit which renders them extremely vulnerable to attack from above - and we had not been hidden long when mallard alarm calls announced the arrival of an osprey. We looked up and saw the male gliding through blue sky as he scanned the water with his yellow eyes. He seemed to be concentrating on one spot, circling several times before folding his wings. He fell like a stone, hurtling through the air at 70 feet a second until at the last moment his talons thrust forward for the kill.

He hit the water with a crash that sent a fountain of spray into the air. As it fell back, and the ripples spread out across the surface of the lochan, pike and osprey were locked in a desperate struggle. The big fish, struck behind the head by eight needle-sharp claws, thrashed its broad tail frantically to break free. The osprey, for its part, unable to lift the pike from the water, found itself being dragged helplessly along the surface in a wide circle. Only his outstretched wings prevented him from being dragged under and drowned, a fate that has befallen more than one osprey in the past. The bird, making a supreme effort, raised his broad wings and with several powerful flaps lifted

the head of the fish from the water, but the pike gave a violent lunge and dragged the osprey back. At last the osprey began to tire of the unequal struggle. He let the fish go and splashed wearily into the air, shaking his waterlogged feathers like a mop before landing heavily on a nearby birch stump.

Twenty minutes later, distant calls from his hungry mate echoed across the glen and he took off, circling up towards the scudding cirrus. Below him the white thread of a tumbling burn spilled down from a corrie lochan, hidden high in the mountains.

As the osprey followed the burn into the hills he disturbed a female goosander which had been hunting for fingerling trout in a peaty pool among the rocks. The goosander grunted with displeasure as she took flight, and circled several times before landing in a magnificent granny pine higher up the burn, where she mysteriously disappeared. We climbed the hill to investigate and eventually discovered a large crack in one of the lateral branches; the mystery was solved. Around the hole a few flecks of down had attached themselves to the rough bark; evidently this was her nest.

The setting she had chosen was idyllic, with steep mountains above and the burn rushing past in a succession of waterfalls, rapids and rocky pools to a distant loch below. Determined to see the fledging of the goosander chicks, we set up a hide in the deep heather opposite the nest and waited.

We had been told that the vulnerable youngsters normally leave during first light, so each day we would climb the hill in the dark, sit in the hide all day and leave only when the sun slid behind the western hills. It was almost midsummer; dawn was at 3.30 am and sunset after 9.00 pm. Tree pipits and ring ousels sang in the long cloudless days and a grey wagtail fed its growing young. Each day we sat and watched the pine's moving shadow marking out the hours, yet time passed quickly, for there seemed no finer place to be.

The osprey's favourite fishing spot was a marshy lochan which nestled among the ancient pines.

On the twelfth morning the vigil was over. The female was unusually excited, quacking loudly as she swam back and forth on the pool below the nest. Soon she flew up to the branch, and out of the crevice appeared the heads of several delightful little goosanderlings. Speckled cream and brown, each with a miniature version of their mother's saw-tooth bill, they were the epitome of the fluffy duckling. But there was little time to admire them. The moment they appeared the female dropped into the heather 20 feet below and the chicks followed, flinging themselves into space.

The female was now extremely excited, quacking loudly and looking anxiously around as she gathered her scattered brood on a rock. A quick head count and they were off into the torrent, to be swept away over the waterfall into the foaming white water below. It was clearly a baptism for which goosander chicks are well prepared, for soon they bobbed to the surface and stayed close to the female as she led them downriver, shooting the rapids as if they had been born to it. Once they had passed the hide and been washed out of sight we raced after them and waited downstream behind a boulder in the river, hidden beneath a camouflage net so as not to be seen by the female.

Within minutes the family bobbed into sight, the female leading her brood through the white water with two chicks riding pillion on her back. One fell off when negotiating a particularly rough stretch of water but paddled to catch up with surprising speed for one so young. Together they shot past in a flurry of bubbles and spray, and within half an hour they had reached the limpid waters of the lochan in the glen below. There the chicks snatched at midge larvae with hungry eagerness. Then, their first meal complete, the female led them to the shore and they fell into a deep sleep.

All six had survived the fall from the tree and come through the white water slalom unscathed and,

though eight is a more usual brood size, the mother's orange feet suggested that she was a young bird and this her first attempt at breeding. Her choice of nest-site high on the hill was also a disadvantage, for it was some way from the favoured feeding spots farther down the glen where the burn widened and small fish were more plentiful. Here the chicks would grow rapidly on their diet of fingerling trout, salmon, eels and minnows, but their predatory habits do not endear them to salmon anglers or gamekeepers, who treat them as vermin. Yet, despite persecution, goosanders are slowly increasing their breeding range.

The goosander first bred in the British Isles in 1871. More recently, the goldeneye, another diving duck, has begun to breed in Scotland. These delightful birds have been common winter visitors from Scandinavia for many years. But since 1970, when the first chicks were discovered, they have slowly colonized the Spey valley. Their normal summer haunts are the coniferous forests of northern Europe, the USSR and North America, where mature forest trees provide good nesting holes and freshwater lakes and rivers offer abundant aquatic insects.

In Scotland the provision of purpose-built nest-boxes by the RSPB and the help of many local people have encouraged an increase to nearly 100 breeding attempts each year, and well over 2,000 goldeneye ducklings have hatched since the first chicks were raised 20 years ago. In this past decade of environmental disasters, it is a relief to be able to turn with hope to a Scottish success, where waterbirds such as goosander, goldeneye and osprey have all substantially increased. Outwardly the situation appears encouraging, but it is worth considering why these species are doing well.

Events in Scandinavia, coupled with deliberations in the European Parliament and the House of Commons make it clear that serious problems lurk

The delightful goldeneye, a diving duck, has recently begun to breed in Scotland.

THE WATER HUNTERS

Trout-catching ospreys share the lochs with eel-loving otters.

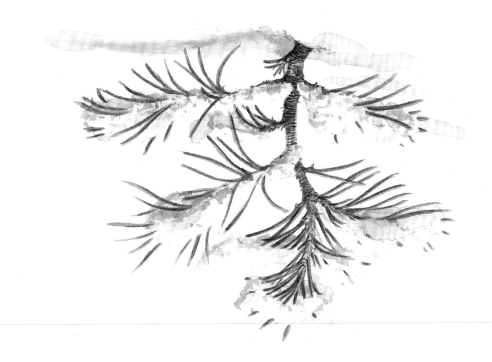

below the surface of our lakes and rivers. Atmospheric pollution over large areas of Britain and Europe has led to serious acidification of waterways and forests. Many Scandinavian lakes and Scottish lochs have lost all their fish life, and it is generally taken for granted that fish-eating birds are badly affected when the numbers of fish in a lake decline. There are undoubtedly fewer ospreys in the worst-affected areas of Europe, with breeding success impaired by eating prey that has been exposed to the metal pollutants that precipitate with what has become known notoriously as acid rain.

Not all the effects are harmful. When fish numbers decline in a loch, the predation pressure on many kinds of aquatic insects decreases and the subsequent abundance of crustaceans and molluscs - the preferred food of the goldeneye - could be one of the reasons why these ducks have increased. Also, increases in acidity are accompanied by an increase in water transparency. For fish-eating birds such as goosanders, which pursue their prey by sight underwater, better vision is compensation for fewer fish. But this is not so for the surface plungers like ospreys, which are limited by the maximum depth they can reach during their

spectacular crash-dives. For them, compensation comes in the form of lochs densely stocked with fat rainbow trout for angling tourists.

So in Scotland at least, the effects of acid rain have been diluted, and the lochans that sparkle between the pines are still brimming with life. The ancient cycle of hunter and hunted remains unbroken: trout and osprey, eel and otter. To watch an otter was always a privilege. We seldom saw them, though often we found their musky spraints by the water margins and saw their broad, five-toed tracks sealed in the mud. But one day, sitting among the pines above our favourite loch, we were thrilled to see the flat, whiskery muzzle of a big dog-otter cleaving the water as he headed for the shore with an eel in his jaws. When he had finished his meal he bounded away into the forest, stopping to spraint on a prominent mound beneath the towering pines: a calling card for other otters on the track between lochan and river. Crows cursed him through the woods and small birds cried in alarm long after he had slipped unseen into the silver Spey. Darkness brings fear, but when the otter hunted seatrout under the rising moon, there was only silence.

CHAPTER SEVEN

Tooth and Claw

As midsummer drew closer, epic sunsets flared across the glens, igniting the orange and salmon-pink trunks of the pines. Later and later the sun sank behind the western hills, each day now separated by only a few hours of eerie half-light in which the dew settled and night slid down into the corries and red-throated divers moaned on the lochans.

At this time of the year it was no hardship to be away to the hill before the sun was up and the dawn chorus just beginning. Entering the forest never failed to arouse a curious sense of anticipation. Who knew what might be waiting in that solitude? As the old trees closed in they stirred dark atavistic memories, as if the wolves and bears of Caledon had never entirely disappeared. But on this particular morning it was not the song of the wolf but the frantic alarm calls of a thrush that interrupted our reveries.

Tits, wrens and tree pipits were adding their own warning voices. Clearly a predator was on the prowl - but what was it? We crept forward, hoping to see a pine marten, but found to our surprise that it was a male red squirrel, caught in the act of robbing the song thrush's nest. The squirrel saw us straight away, and despite all our attempts at concealment, and fled with his rufous tail plumed out behind, using the aerial walkways of the forest canopy to put a safe distance between us.

Three sky-blue eggs, each with a scattering of black freckles, lay safe and warm in the nest's clay cup. Only the fourth had been eaten, with half its shell lying where the squirrel had dropped it on the ground beneath. It seemed that we had interrupted the squirrel's breakfast just in time. But next morning, when we returned, the nest was empty.

Although it is common knowledge that red squirrels sometimes raid nests, such behaviour has seldom been observed - making what followed all the more extraordinary. Later that morning, having left the deserted thrush's nest, we had not gone far before we heard the familiar 'pink-pink' alarm calls of a chaffinch together with a host of other scolding voices - siskin, willow warbler and tree-creeper.

Once more, to our amazement, the culprit was a squirrel. Could it be the same animal, we wondered? Certainly it was a male. At any rate he seemed to have learned that the birds' agitated behaviour indicated the likely presence of a nest not far away. As we watched, he began a methodical search of the surrounding trees and bushes, which was rewarded after about 20 minutes by the discovery of a chaffinch's nest with four young, lodged high up in the crotch of a pine. The distressed parents could only look on helplessly as he proceeded to eat the nestlings one by one, nibbling their naked pink bodies as if they were so many sticks of rock. Then, adding a final indignity, he settled comfortably in the fork of the tree with the empty nest supporting his fat little belly, and went to sleep.

These two incidents vividly illustrate the Jekyll-and-Hyde nature of these elfin creatures. Attractive they may be, with their tufted ears and elegantly curling tails; but during the nesting season they can also become efficient little opportunists. It also taught us that listening for birds' alarm calls was one of the surest ways of locating these shy animals. Even when we managed to track them down, they possessed an extraordinary ability to vanish, Houdini-like, slipping out of sight around the far side of a tree trunk or freezing on a high branch until we had gone.

In Britain the red squirrel has an ancient pedigree. It reached this country around 9000 BC, following the march of the pines from Europe after the Ice Age, only to be marooned here when the ice melted and the North Sea rose, cutting off all retreat.

In Scotland, the destruction of the Great Wood of Caledon brought the species close to extinction. Yet somehow they survived and increased to the point where, at one time, hundreds of red squirrels were sent south to be sold for food in London's Leadenhall Market. In 1903 the Highland Squirrel Club was formed to cull their numbers on the great estates, which it did so successfully that 80,000 red squirrels were killed in 30 years. But by then nature, too, had lent a hand and the population crashed. The reason for their demise is unclear. It may have been an epidemic; or it could have been related to the arrival in Britain of the North American grey squirrel, first introduced in

*Two incidents involving red squirrels vividly illustrate the
Jekyll-and-Hyde nature of these elfin creatures.*

1876 in Cheshire. Since then the larger and more vigorous grey squirrel has established itself at the expense of the native red. Today, driven from all but a few haunts in southern Britain, the red squirrel is still declining except in places such as the relic woods of Caledon, which could well become its last wild refuge.

Red squirrels give birth any time between February and July. The youngsters we saw just emerging from their drey in June would have been conceived in the depths of winter. Mated after a lengthy chase through the treetops by her suitor, their mother may have built two or three dreys before choosing one as a breeding nest and lining it snugly with grass. Here, some time in February or March, she had produced her litter. The young, usually three or four in number, are born blind, naked and helpless. With their thin hairless tails, they look more like rats at this time of their lives and are utterly dependent upon their mother.

Inside the natal drey they grow quickly. At three weeks they are fully furred, and a week later open their eyes. Another four weeks pass before they emerge from the drey for the first time to explore their treetop world, and at 10 weeks they are fully weaned. In these early days the young squirrels are at their most vulnerable and stay close to home, never straying more than 200 yards from the safety of the drey. But they become increasingly bold and adventurous, indulging in experimental bark-chewing to keep their teeth down and chasing each other in dizzy games of tag with their mother.

We watched one family inspecting an old drey in a stag-headed pine. The young squirrels approached it cautiously until one youngster, more curious than the rest, finally plucked up courage and with a flick of his tail disappeared into the nest - only to appear moments later vigorously scratching himself with his hind feet. The old drey must have been infested with fleas, which had been waiting for just such an opportunity!

Everywhere under the trees we would find the chewed and discarded cores of pine cones - the most obvious clues which revealed the widespread presence of red squirrels. Although they also thrive in deciduous woods of oak and hazel, the reds are among the oldest inhabitants of the boreal forest, the vast coniferous woodlands of the cold north, of which the Caledonian forest is now their British stronghold.

Among the Scots pines they thrive on the bountiful harvests of pine seeds, which mature in the autumn and fall to the ground the following spring. Once on the ground and released from their protective cones, the seeds are eagerly snapped up by mice and small birds. But the agile squirrels are able to reach the seeds before they fall and remain active all winter, plundering the trees of their precious cones.

Watching the youngsters at play, leaping fearlessly from branch to branch or scampering headlong down the tall trunks, it was sad to think that three years is the average life span for a wild red squirrel. A few would be taken by eagles and pine martens. Others would die of starvation or disease. Even in a normal year, when pine cones were abundant, their life was an endless hunt for food, and the Highland summer could be a lean time for squirrels. Maybe that was why, during this particular year, they hunted so diligently for eggs and nestlings; and why, as we discovered, not even the nests of the giant capercaillie were safe.

We arrived at the caper hide at four in the morning to find the hen sitting tight and everything, including her beautiful mottled plumage, beaded with a fine drizzle. We, too, sat tight in the chill of the dawn, watching and waiting. The soaking woods were quiet and sombre, the distant hills lost in low cloud. Suddenly, at seven o'clock, the beginning of the red squirrel's most active hour, there was the sound of branches being lightly shaken, followed by the scratch of sharp claws on bark. Almost at once a squirrel

The female capercaillie began to move deeper into the forest.

TOOTH AND CLAW

*Everywhere under the trees we would find the chewed
and discarded cores of pine cones.*

appeared, coming jerkily head-first down the trunk of the tree immediately behind the sitting caper.

The squirrel was very alert, tufted ears cocked and feathery tail twitching nervously. There seemed little doubt that it had seen the sitting bird. Maybe it had heard the chicks, which had hatched only the previous day. The capercaillie froze. By now the squirrel was on the ground and still the big brown bird stayed still.

The squirrel grew bolder. It came forward and began to circle the nest, sidling closer until it was no more than three feet away. This was too much for the caper. She puffed out her feathers, extended her neck and began to emit a low, menacing purr as her head weaved from side to side, facing her adversary. Only then did the squirrel back away and make off into the trees. A squirrel is unlikely to pose a real threat to a sitting capercaillie but perhaps this animal had simply never seen the giant grouse at such close quarters before. At any rate it was a fascinating encounter.

An hour later, although the day was still grey and overcast, the capercaillie chicks emerged and began to run in and out of the hen's breast feathers. Eventually the mother stood up and walked slowly from the nest with her youngsters trailing behind her. She was clearly very hungry and began to feed almost at once, occasionally pausing to utter little muted contact calls to keep the chicks together.

Towards midday the cloud cover began to lift and the sun broke through to disperse the dampness of the morning. By now it had become quite warm, almost sultry, and the mother caper and her fluffy chicks began to move deeper into the forest. Soon we could no longer see them, but we could still hear the anxious hen softly calling above the insistent summer voices of wood pigeons lower down the valley.

By now it was not only the birds of Caledon who had youngsters to feed. During one of our daily forays into the woods we caught a faint whisper of sound, as

A juvenile great spotted woodpecker peered at the ancient forest for the first time.

*Entering the forest never failed to arouse a
curious sense of anticipation.*

THE GREAT WOOD OF CALEDON

For most of its life the pine marten is a solitary hunter, travelling many miles each night.

of small feet pattering on dry rock, and turned round with the uncanny feeling that we were being watched. Sure enough, an animal the size of a small, thin cat was staring at us with bright inquisitive eyes from a tumble of boulders between the trees. Its fur was a thick, rich brown except for the rims of its ears and its bib, which were creamy yellow. It returned our gaze with no sign of fear, rising up on its hind legs to obtain a better view of us. For a moment it stood there, nostrils twitching as it sought our scent. Then without warning it turned and ran, rippling over the rocks with its long bushy tail flowing out behind, and vanished down a deep crevice.

The pine marten is essentially a night prowler, a moonlight assassin, slipping through the forest shadows in search of mice and voles; but this particular animal, we discovered later, was a female with three young kits to feed, and it was their hungry appetites which now drove her to hunt in daylight, risking death in the clutches of her only true natural enemy - the golden eagle. For us it was a lucky encounter. Pine martens are among the rarest of all British mammals, seldom seen except as a pair of silver-green eyes caught late at night in a car's headlights. Even here, in its most secure stronghold in the pine forests of the north-western Highlands, such a sighting was a privilege.

1,000 years ago it was a different story. Then the pine marten was quite common in Scotland and widespread over much of Britain. In the Middle Ages it was prized for its lustrous pelt, which lacked the polecat's rank odour, giving the pine marten one of its numerous alternative names - sweet-mart. Yet still the species thrived, in spite of the fur hunters, until the loss of its forest habitat combined with the unwelcome attentions of 19th-century gamekeepers drove it from its southern haunts.

By the late 1800s the pine marten had all but vanished from England. It retained a lingering presence in the Lake District, and the Welsh knew that *bele'r coed* - the cat of the trees - still haunted the lonely dingles of Snowdonia. Even in Scotland its range continued to contract, until it was virtually confined to the remote and rainswept Highlands beyond the Great Glen. Here, among the mountains and woods of Wester Ross, in the roadless wilderness that sprawls beneath the gaunt and glittering quartzite screes of Beinn Eighe and the corries of Torridon, the *taghan*, as it is known in Gaelic, made its last stand.

Today the pine marten is still a rare animal, but the planting of new conifers and a more enlightened attitude towards predators has enabled the species to spread south and reoccupy many of its former Scottish haunts, including wide areas of Speyside and Argyll. Even so, there are still some keepers who refer to the pine marten by its old pre-war name - the 'scourge of the glen'.

For most of its life the pine marten is a solitary hunter, with a home range extending over as much as 10 square miles of hill and forest. Every night it travels many miles, marking its territorial frontiers with musky signals, leaving scats overlaid with anal secretions to signposts its regular pathways.

It climbs by clasping the trunk with its front paws, digging in its razor-sharp claws and then pushing itself up with both hind legs together in a series of quick jerky movements. Once aloft in the pinewood canopy it is both fearless and sure-footed.

Who can outclimb the squirrel
But the weasel of the trees?
Who can outrun the roe deer
And catch the hare with ease?

So ran the words of a 19th-century hunting song; yet the pine marten is not a true arboreal dweller. Nor are red squirrels by any means its favourite prey. Crag marten or stone marten would be a more fitting name for this giant weasel, which spends most of its time on the ground searching for voles, beetles, frogs, bees' nests and autumn berries, even spent salmon washed down from their spawning redds. It is also renowned for possessing a sweet tooth. Mike Tomkies, the naturalist and wildlife author who spent 13 years in the Western Highlands, found that pine martens would even come to his windowsill to feed on hand-held tidbits of bread and raspberry jam. But it is in the 'vole years' - when the short-tailed field voles experience a population explosion - that pine martens grow fat and prosper.

For the female we had surprised in the woods, the abundance of voles was especially welcome. The three young kits she had produced beneath the hollowed roots of a hillside pine were growing fast. When they had been born in April each of them weighed just two ounces. Now they were almost as big as she was.

Pine martens produce only one litter a year. The female had been mated the previous summer, a noisy and violent affair more like a fight to the death than a love-match, in which the pair had rolled over and over, snarling and yammering at one another as the male strove to pin her down. Although their union had been consummated in late August, delayed implantation had held back the time of birth until spring, when hunting was easier. For at least six weeks the kits had kept to the den while their eyes opened and their fur coats grew thick and soft. Now, although fully weaned, they were still dependent upon their mother and would stay together as a family until the autumn. We watched one of them, easily distinguishable from the mother by its paler, fluffier coat, sniffing in search of prey. Already its movements were quick and bright as a snake as it flowed through the heather towards a bank where voles had left tell-tale tunnels through the grass.

Many voles would die that summer to feed the marten's family; and not only voles. A few days earlier we had found the remains of two crested tits' nests - both showing unmistakable signs of breaking and entering. We could not be sure, but the evidence seemed to point to the pine martens as the culprits. Who else could have dug so deep into the dead wood to carry off the nestlings? But the wary voles were a more elusive quarry and it would take older, wiser hunters than the inexperienced young martens to catch them napping.

CHAPTER EIGHT

Cat and Mouse

'I have heard their wild and unearthly cry echo far into the quiet night as they answer and call to each other.' So wrote Charles St John, the famous 19th-century sportsman, when describing the Scottish race of the European wildcat. The cat he wrote about was no suburban tabby, 'gone bush', but a true species, with an ancestry stretching back to the Ice Age. But for centuries it has been treated as vermin, due perhaps to its mythological powers of killing. Even naturalists such as Thomas Pennant, writing 200 years ago, perpetuated the stories. 'This animal may be called the British tiger', it is the fiercest and most destructive beast we have, making dreadful havoc among our poultry, lambs and kids.'

There are few landowners and keepers who now believe the wildcat capable of killing lambs, but its reputation for ferocity still lingers. As recently as 1977 a naturalist writing in a national newspaper described how 'utterly fearless they are, likely to spring at your throat like a tiger'. Such behaviour would be purely defensive, for the wildcat is the shyest of creatures, doing its utmost to avoid contact with man. But if cornered, the wildcat will indeed fight like a tiger. Charles St John described how he once stumbled on one while walking his three terriers in a glen. 'I never saw an animal fight so desperately or one which was so difficult to kill. If a tame cat has nine lives, a wildcat must have a dozen.'

He gave no justification for his act of violence, but malevolence towards the wildcat was widespread, especially when the 19th-century sporting estates employed thousands of gamekeepers in order to protect their quarry species. All predators were treated as vermin - on some estates they still are - and wildcats, once common in England, Wales and Scotland, were trapped, snared and shot in such large numbers that they were wiped out from all but the remote fastnesses of the western Highlands. By the turn of the century naturalists were predicting their extinction in Britain but a few survivors hid among the crags and ancient pines until the Great War drew the keepers away, allowing wildcats to increase until they are once again becoming abundant over much of the Scottish

Highlands. But there is concern among scientists and conservationists that the genetic purity of the Scottish wildcat is becoming diluted by hybridization. The domestic cat is believed to have descended from the African wildcat, and wildcats and domestic cats are thus so closely related that they are capable of mating and producing fertile offspring. Many wildcats now show the tell-tale signs (white blotches and a longer tapering tail) of amorous adventures with their domestic cousins, and this has contributed to their increase. Re-afforestation has also assisted their recovery, for dense woodland provides refuge against adverse weather and hostile keepers as well as affording thick cover for hunting. Rabbits form by far the largest part of their diet, and the arrival of myxomatosis may have helped some wildcats by providing easy meals. Like the pine marten, they also catch large numbers of small rodents and, less frequently, small birds.

In order to observe their hunting technique, we built a huge enclosure in a seldom-visited corner of the ancient forest and released in it a pair of wildcats from a wildlife park. They seemed blissfully happy in their own private wilderness, settling down to a natural routine among the dense stands of pine, birch and rowan. Under the trees lay a thick carpet of heather, juniper, grass and moss, beneath which rocky caves were concealed among twisted tree roots. There were even a number of fallen trees, ripped out by past storms, and the cats loved to sleep in the sun on top of their upturned root plates.

Despite the fact that wildcats are now widely distributed in the Highlands they are seldom seen, even by sharp-eyed keepers, and then usually only in their Land-Rover headlights. This elusiveness is evidently an essential part of the wildcat's character, for even our two cats, bred in captivity, proved very difficult to see. We would sit hidden for hours before a prickling sensation on the back of the neck made us aware that we were being watched, and even then a careful search with binoculars was needed before the slits of suspicious greenish eyes could be detected beneath a shadowy tangle of roots. Robins, tits and chaffinches could come and go freely between the

Chaffinches would scold the wildcats from a safe distance.

enclosing wire mesh and would scold the cats from a safe distance as they stalked voles in the grey half-light of dawn or dusk - their most active time of day.

One warm July evening, just after the sun had flared and faded behind the darkening pines, we became aware of a wood mouse in a small clearing. It was quite well hidden but its tell-tale nibbling had alerted the female wildcat. Her flattened ears appeared first, slowly rising from behind a fallen pine. Her eyes were narrowed in concentration as she froze, half hidden, trying to pinpoint the rustling. The wood mouse was some 10 feet away, feeding on a spray of blaeberry, and to reach it the wildcat had to climb slowly over the fallen tree trunk, her body flattened like a big cat stalking African game. Closing on her prey, she sneaked swiftly between heather and blaeberry, until she was within striking distance, when she paused briefly, licking her lips in anticipation, as if in a Tom and Jerry cartoon, while her hindquarters

tensed and quivered. The mouse stopped feeding and, though apparently unaware of the danger, began to move off. In an instant the cat pounced. Claws and teeth came together as the cat came down on the mouse with a deadly thump. There was no toying with her victim like a house cat; no games of cat and mouse. A wildcat kills to eat, and ours quickly slunk off through the trees to her rocky den with the mouse gripped firmly in her jaws.

Her den was in a small cave among a mossy jumble of rocks, hidden from even the most careful searcher by a tangle of fern, juniper and pine. We waited quietly behind the rocks. Twenty minutes later the wildcat cautiously emerged and jumped on to the trunk of a fallen pine, exposing an impressive array of sharp teeth as she yawned and stretched, digging her front claws into the peeling bark. As she walked along the length of the trunk her 11 black body stripes stood out boldly on her grey-brown coat. Although

*A careful search was needed before the slits of suspicious green eyes
could be detected beneath a shadowy tangle of roots.*

superficially similar to a domestic tabby, a wildcat is more powerfully built and roughly one third larger.

Our male was a magnificent specimen measuring more than 40 inches from pink nose to furry tail tip and weighing 19 pounds - a true heavyweight champion. The black stripes on his head gave him a fierce, tigerish appearance and his tail, his best distinguishing feature, was short and bushy, with five black rings and a blunt black tip. He looked superb and, when surprised, could respond with an impressive display of explosive aggression. We were looking for him in the enclosure one day when he suddenly sprang out from beneath a juniper, teeth bared, ears flattened and green eyes ablaze. His unexpected appearance, combined with his spitting hiss and the thump of his paws on the ground, made us jump back in alarm. His thick fur stood on end and he growled at us, a menacing rumble from deep down in his chest making us back off even farther. Then he turned and slipped away into the undergrowth.

Normally he was extremely shy and seldom seen, despite us feeding him rabbit each day. The female, on the other hand, allowed us to approach quite close, though she, too, retained her underlying suspicion of man, a fear deeply ingrained by centuries of persecution. On one particular day we had been sitting close to her for several hours when we heard the distant noise of a car door slamming and the sound of voices. They were a long way off, but she immediately flattened herself into the heather and within seconds had melted into invisibility. Watching her then it struck us how impossible it would be to stalk a wildcat in the forest, however silently one moved.

One June dawn we were tracking a family of capercaillie which had just fledged from their nest below a granny pine. The female was clucking softly to her eight small chicks, keeping them together as they fed on insects, when she suddenly became tense. Her feathers tightened, her neck stretched, and a change of

The male redstart hesitated before taking food to his young.

CAT AND MOUSE

Wet summers prove harmful to capercaillie chicks
and even to the forest itself.

*In a few places, pink twinflowers add their
delicate beauty to the forest floor.*

note had the chicks scurrying for cover. Redstarts, tree pipits, siskins and crested tits gathered to scold an unseen predator, and from its movements, traced by watching the birds, it was obvious that the capercaillie chicks were being stalked by a wildcat. Despite much stealthy creeping, the cat failed to catch a chick and eventually slunk away into the shadowy forest, with the alarm calls of birds ringing in its ears. We had failed to catch so much as a glimpse of it, though the chances of seeing a wildcat do improve each year. Persecution continues, but recent protection in the Wildlife and Countryside Act will help this wildest relic of the ancient forest survive and prosper.

Not so the capercaillie. Although wildcats undoubtedly take capercaillie chicks, far more suffer as a result of the uncertain Scottish climate. The critical time is the week of hatching in early June. If the capercaillie chicks become cold and wet they will die, and a series of poor years has left the capercaillie population at a seriously low ebb. The situation is made even worse by the loss of so much prime forest.

Wet summers have also proved harmful to the forest itself, for waterlogged ground deters regeneration and kills trees. In some areas, especially in the wetter west, the forest floor is suffering a creeping invasion of spongy sphagnum moss. Tear up two handfuls and you can wring a cup of water from it. And that, to the Scots pine, spells disaster; for the accumulated wetness is insidious, steadily loosening the clenched roots until, in a gale, even the strongest tree will lurch from its socket like a rotten molar.

Several centuries ago, a climatic change destroyed huge areas of forest and reduced the altitude at which trees could grow by 500 feet. Now all that remains of those great pines are their bleached skeletons, buried in a black morass of sphagnum and peat. Yet in some wet hollows the trees have survived. With their growth inhibited by their waterlogged roots, even 100-year-old veterans barely reach 10 feet and their trunks and branches, contorted and pollarded by the nibbling of animals, give them the look of Japanese bonsai trees. In summer, dragonflies glitter above the pools and the bogs are carpeted with insect-eating plants - sundews and butterworts.

The drier forest, too, has its special flowers, some of which occur only among the ancient pines. Specialist orchids such as the lesser twayblade and creeping ladies' tresses push shyly up to the sun. Shady spots are illuminated by the tiny white stars of the one-flowered wintergreen, a rare plant whose delicate flowers give it a nickname: St Olaf's candlestick. In a few places, pink twinflowers add their own frail beauty to the forest floor and, as autumn approaches, cowberries, bilberries and bearberries ripen to provide a colourful harvest for forest animals and birds.

As the Highland nights draw in and the first frosts shiver down the glens, dawn mists hang in the woods and the chill moisture encourages the forest floor to sprout a variety of fungi: bright red splashes of the white-spotted, hallucinogenic fly agaric, a yellow slime fungi, and a pretty spore-spreader named *Lycogala epidendron*. The fungi provide food for red squirrels, who collect them in the autumn and stuff them into crevices in the fissured bark of pines, where they dry to provide a winter cache.

Crested tits also prepare for winter, laying in food as a provision against harsh weather. During late summer they catch many pine looper caterpillars and, like all good housekeepers, process the food for storage. By eating the heads and removing part of the gut, the tits may actually help to preserve the caterpillars, which are then stored away in the lower branches, hidden under lichen or even stuck on with saliva. Unfortunately, crested tits cannot remember where they have hidden the food. Tests have revealed that marsh tits have a 'memory window' of only a day, and great tits only five minutes. But at least when winter comes the food will be there, waiting to be re-discovered, and these possible storage spots are where crested tits concentrate their search.

Storing food is vital to crested tits, for bad weather is a killer of small birds and Highland winters can be severe. Crested tits try to avoid the worst effects of cold nights by communal roosting, high in the tree canopy, but numbers are few. The most ever found huddled together was a roost of 14. For the small birds of the pine forest, the crested tits, chaffinches, tree creepers, siskins and goldcrests, the autumn days are spent feeding in large parties of mixed species, travelling widely, even visiting bird tables, where crested tits have been seen eating haggis.

So autumn is a time of frantic activity, accompanied by a flowering of the forest as swathes of mauve heather flow down from the hills. The birches turn colour - yellow flames among the blue-green pines - and far above, the hills echo to the bugling bark of rutting stags. Their primeval voices ring out like a summons. The year's final act is about to begin.

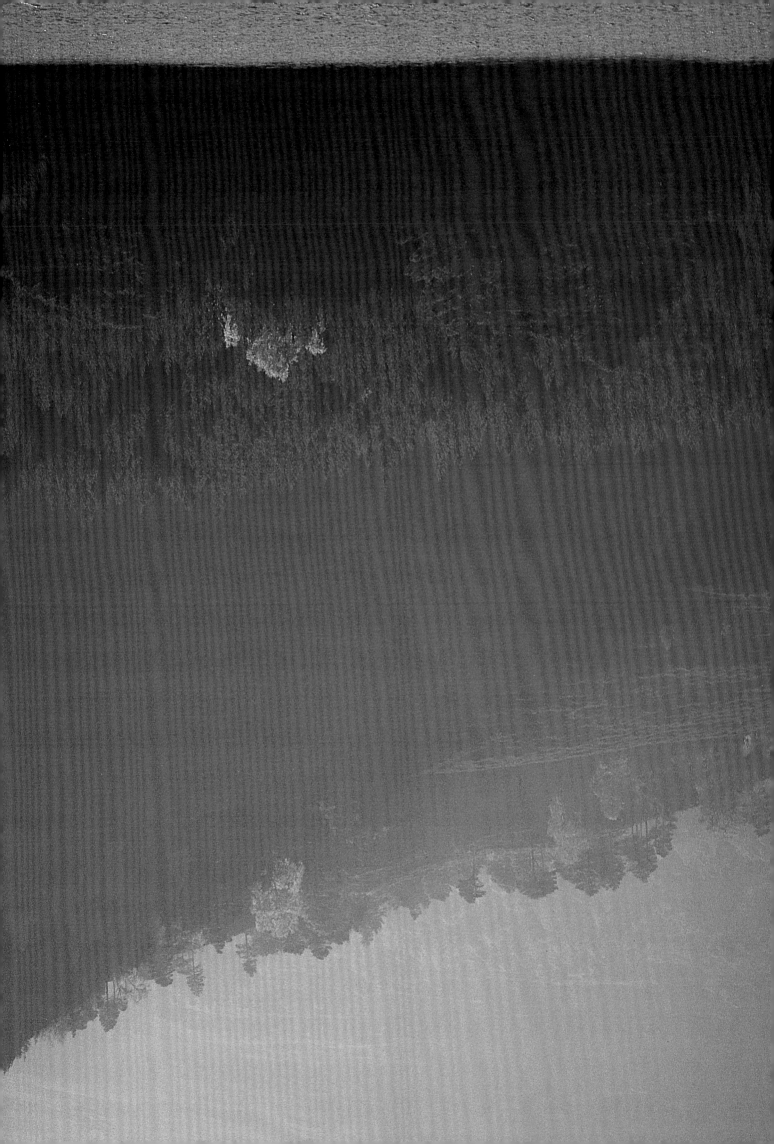

CHAPTER NINE

Monarchs of the Glen

In October the weather began to break. Great blustery gales came rampaging out of the west, churning the lochs into a turmoil of white water and racing on over the hills to go crashing through the pinewoods. Between the storms, clear nights were followed by sharp frosts. Bracken rusted on the hillsides; birches glowed gold in the glens. The seasons were changing; the days growing shorter. Lit by the flaring colours of autumn leaves, the Highland year was going down in a blaze of glory.

In the pinewoods it was a time of redoubled activity as birds and animals fed and fattened or hoarded food to see them through the long winter siege. Red squirrels fiercely defended their territories, chasing out intruders who might steal the precious fungi, seeds and cones without which they could not survive.

The ospreys, their broods safely reared and on the wing, had forsaken the estuaries where they had taken to hunting and set out again on their immense odyssey to the warm south, where they would spend the winter fishing in the shallow seas and mangrove swamps of the Gambia. Their treetop eyries, the scene of so much noise and activity during the summer, were now empty, hostages to the winter storms.

The summer songbirds, too, had long since fled south, leaving the woodlands strangely silent. But autumn brought the return of old and familiar sounds that stirred the blood and made the heart leap to hear them again. A wild music fell from the clouds. The greylag geese were back, filling the sky with their exultant clamourings as they broke formation, spilling the air from their broad pinions to come tumbling down into the Insh marshes on the floodplain of the River Spey.

Above the woods, where the heather had faded to the colour of burnt cork, a desolation of rock and peat bog reached up into the trailing clouds. From everywhere came the trickle of water dribbling out of the hills.

Up in the lonely glens and amphitheatres of the high corries, the red stags had gathered to contest the right to mate. Caught up in the throes of the rut, they thrashed their antlers in the heather and wallowed in the peat hags until their thick winter coats were black and glistening. Thickset and in their prime, with shaggy manes and spreading antlers, the lords of the rut - grizzled veterans of seven or eight years in the hills - thrust out their muzzles and roared like lions. Their breath smoked in the frosty air as their deep-throated bellowings rang out across the glens, to be answered by other, distant, challengers whose voices were flung back by the dark crags into hollows in the hills.

In October the full-grown stags are a magnificent sight, standing four feet high at the shoulder, with a spread of antlers that may grow to around 28 inches. Their thick winter coats are no longer red but a dull donkey brown that blends with the dun colours of the dying moors. All summer long they live apart from the hinds, yearlings and calves, roaming the hills in bachelor groups and keeping to their own traditional feeding ranges. But in autumn, the rut brings stags and hinds together as rival males grunt and groan as they strive to hold harems of mature breeding females.

The roaring of the stags plays a vital part in the process of natural selection. With swollen neck and bristling mane, each stag tries to out-roar its rivals. Sometimes two males will walk side by side, matching pace with pace as they size each other up. But when roaring fails to intimidate, fighting takes place and the two combatants come together with a furious clash of antlers, each animal heaving and shoving to gain the advantage. Inevitably, many fights result in serious injuries. Broken antlers are common, and it is not unknown for the antlers of two fighting stags to become so inextricably locked that both animals die.

What drives them to fever pitch is the fact that each hind is sexually receptive for no more than a day. With so little time for mating, the anxious stags are forced to remain on constant alert, chasing off other males and preventing their hinds from straying. A veteran stag may, if he is lucky, round up and hold captive a harem of up to a score of hinds. When they come into season, the hinds advertise their readiness by emitting a scent which causes the stag to chase them

The greylag geese were back, filling the sky with their exultant clamourings.

and sniff their rumps. The pair of them then lick and nuzzle each other before mating takes place.

If the mating is successful, the calves will be born in June. A good hind may produce as many as 10 calves in her lifetime, and few fail to breed at all. But first the herds must survive the long Highland winter, and October seldom fails to bring the first flurries of snow to the high tops. By November the upper hillsides above the woods can be deep in snow. Mountain hares and ptarmigan wear white for winter, hiding from the eagles which patrol the skies from dawn to dusk.

In summer the red deer cling to the high tops, shunning the dangerous world of man in the glens below and avoiding the torment of biting insects. Yet even there, feeding on heather, grasses and lichens in the lonely haunts of grouse and golden plover, they remain continually alert, with ears cocked and black noses constantly twitching as they sift the air for scent,

and trot away at the most distant glimpse of a hill-walker, rocking over the peat hummocks and spongy mosses to pause briefly on the skyline before they vanish out of sight.

As winter approaches, the red deer grow bolder and seem to lose their shyness, coming down from the hills at dusk to browse among the outlying pines of the upper forests. And when the weather grows harder, when the lochans freeze from shore to shore, when the wind-blown snow forms blue cornices along the crests and summits of the mountains and icicles hang from the eagles' crag, the deer are driven to seek sanctuary in the last welcoming tracts of the Caledonian pine forest.

The deer and the pines are bound by an ancient lineage, having lived together since the dawn of history. The red deer of the Scottish Highlands are no different from the animals painted by the palaeolithic cave-dwellers of Lascaux in France 15,000 years ago; and when the pines spread north into Scotland as the

Red deer are driven to seek sanctuary in the last welcoming tracts of the Caledonian pine forest.

glaciers retreated, the roaring of the stags must have been one of the first sounds to break the frozen silence of the Ice Age.

Scots pine shoots and seedlings are the red deer's favourite food, confirming what many scientists now believe - that red deer are primarily browsers, forest dwellers who have taken to grazing only since they were driven from the woodlands and forced to forage in the open hills.

In the ancient and undisturbed forest of long ago, the red deer must have been a keystone species, playing a vital role in the overall shaping of the woodlands. In those days the wolf - their chief natural predator - would have helped to control their numbers. But the last wolf was killed in 1743. The forests have all but vanished and the deer herds are now greater than at any time in their history. The problem today is too many deer and not enough Caledonian pine forest to harbour them through the

winter. The result is that the hungry deer are preventing the trees from regenerating, and their chomping teeth and destructive habits pose perhaps the most serious threat to the future of these native pinewoods.

Two hundred years ago the number of red deer in the Scottish Highlands was probably fewer than 10,000; but the rise of sport shooting in Victorian times encouraged landowners to increase the size of their herds. Today some 300,000 deer roam across the hills and moorland, most of it owned by about 250 private estates for whom deer stalking is big business. This involves professional stalkers who will lead their clients on the hill and select the beast to be killed - with sportsmen prepared to pay up to £7,000 for a good trophy.

The shootable stags are killed in the autumn. In all, 15,000 or more stags will be shot each year, and as many hinds culled by stalkers in the winter. Yet still

Like grey ghosts from the dim past, the red deer faded away between the pines.

MONARCHS OF THE GLEN

the numbers of deer have proliferated - doubling in the past 30 years to create serious problems of over-grazing. A recent run of exceptionally cold, wet winters has resulted in a Highland tragedy, with deer starving to death in their thousands. There is no doubt that the weather has played an important part, but the Red Deer Commission says that the main reason is inadequate culling.

According to the Commission, estates have been failing to cull their stocks of hinds in sufficient numbers to keep the balance. Swayed by the revenue to be derived from their trophy stags, they have allowed the herds to grow too big. With too many hungry mouths to feed, the deer cannot sustain themselves through the lean winter months on the meagre Highland tundra.

To make matters worse, when blizzards drive the deer down from the hills in search of food and shelter they find the woodlands fenced off for forestry. With nowhere else to go, they must survive as best they can in the open country, much of which, by the cruellest irony, still goes by the archaic name of 'deer forest'.

As is nature's way, the first to die are the young, the old, the sick and the lame. Some, having battled through deep snowdrifts to reach the safety of the forests, collapse and die against the wire which denies them refuge among the trees. Others, weakened by months of starvation and bone-chilling weather, succumb to the insidious burrowings of liver flukes, lungworms and warble fly larvae, and become mired in peat bogs, or simply freeze to death in the night, to be found next day beneath a mantle of crows or to become carrion for eagles and hill foxes. But the majority struggle on: the proud antlered stags, the smaller 'knobbers' or 'staggies' with their puny, goat-like horns, the gangling calves and, most precious of all, the pregnant hinds who carry the future of the herds inside them. They will ensure that the deer continue to keep watch from the hills, a part of Scotland as old as the running of the salmon and the returning grey geese.

The year had come full circle. Now, once more, we stood in the winter woods with the daylight fading, the snow slanting down and the deer drifting soundlessly among the trees. The wind had died but the snow fell more heavily than ever, smothering the forest floor in smooth, knee-deep billows. Soft, fat flakes clung to the flanks of the deer, matting their heavy manes and freckling their black muzzles as their antlered heads swung round towards us. For a moment they stood there, solemn and unmoving except for the occasional twitch of an ear. Then, like grey ghosts from the dim past when wolves might have trailed them through the Great Wood of Caledon, they faded away between the pines, leaving us alone in the frost-crackling dusk.

Pink Pine cone.

3rd year cone.

♂ pollen flowers
early June 89

CHAPTER TEN
A Future for Caledon

'To stand amongst the ancient pines is to feel the past.' So wrote an eminent forester 30 years ago, and even now we can still experience this sense of excitement.

Looking east over the pines from the top of a glacial moraine, the view gives us a glimpse into history. Under our feet crunch the heaped gravels of the last Ice Age and above us tower 300-year-old pines. Just 30 generations of these veterans take us back to the time when we could have watched great ice floes carving this unique landscape.

Today, the vast expanse of Abernethy still stretches to the far horizon. Beyond rise the hillsides where the pioneers of future forests might advance towards the summit of Cairngorm, shimmering invitingly in the crisp dawn light. This is how the forest has been since the Ice Age shaped these hills - timeless, eternal.

The view to the west is different. Here the history of man's impact on the forest is graphically exposed. The broad strath of the River Spey has been a thoroughfare for man since the exploration of the north began more than 5,000 years ago. Stone axes would have been the first tools to chip away at the Great Wood, followed by bronze ones. Then, 2,500 years ago, the iron axes of the Celts would have exposed more of the river's banks. The Picts followed - even the Romans explored this natural gateway to the north - and all the while the forest was felled to provide fuel, fields and building materials. Much of Strathspey still echoes these activities, with a patchwork of farms and forests, the conifer plantations confined to the less fertile ground and the surrounding hills.

Spread out below us was Garten Wood, part of the RSPB's famous Loch Garten Reserve and the extensive Abernethy forest. Their senior warden in Speyside is Stewart Taylor, a friend for many years, who joined us to describe the changes inflicted on this wood before the Society bought it.

Dropping down off the glacial moraine, we passed under many pine skeletons, the legacy of a huge fire that swept through the forest in the early 1960s. The forest was then clear-felled, but one area survived, protected from both fire and machinery by a surrounding bog. This magical patch of ancient forest is like a secret place, hidden from the outside world by a dense strip of small pines. Forcing our way through was like parting theatre curtains into another, older, world. Enormous trees with huge trunks supporting widespread branches grew among a graveyard of fallen giants. These veterans had lain undisturbed for so long that 20-year-old birches grew out of their upturned roots. Others, though fallen, were still drawing enough moisture for growth to continue, proving that old age can persist a long time before death.

During the 1960s, foresters tried to drain this boggy otherworld in order to plant sitka spruce, that fast-growing exotic conifer, and beyond the ancient forest the contrast between the richness of the old and the poverty of the new was striking. Most of Garten Wood was a monotonous plantation before the RSPB bought it, but, undaunted, they have implemented an imaginative management policy to turn a plantation into rich woodland.

Stewart aims to recover the total infrastructure of a native pinewood, so as well as removing the sitka spruce, much of the plantation has been irregularly thinned, creating everything from open to dense pine stands, with even heavier thinning around well-developed trees. Let the light in and the plant-rich understorey will develop; there will be space for pine regeneration and room for broad-leaved trees such as birch, hazel, sallow and rowan. Stewart is also damming drains to re-create forest bogs for some of the rarer Highland insects, though the remaining ancient areas will be left to develop naturally, as befits our woodland heritage.

This far-sighted forest management looks not just five or 10 years ahead, but half a century away and more. Already results are promising, and a nature trail explains the ecology and provides easy access for the public. Unfortunately this encourages inappropriate recreational use, and some say nature reserves should be for wildlife, not for walkers of dogs and cross-country skiers. So the RSPB is faced with a dilemma, and one whose relevance

Just 30 generations of these veterans take us back to the time
when ice floes carved this unique landscape.

extends far beyond the boundaries of Garten Wood and Abernethy.

How does conservation come to terms with the need to alert people to environmental threats, or ask for their sympathy and financial support and then cope with the influx of those who have been encouraged to take an interest? And does the media help or hinder? Wildlife films have undoubtedly contributed to man's awareness of global problems and created a climate that has allowed the green movement to flourish. On a smaller scale, however, does a film or book that seeks to protect the native pine forest contribute to its conservation or accelerate its decline?

When the RSPB took the bold step of deciding to buy Abernethy Forest Reserve, they appealed to their members for a million pounds. The response was superb, and in no time this magnificent remnant of the ancient forest was protected for ever. Publicity *was* necessary to raise the funds and, naturally, many who contributed were keen to visit the land they had helped to buy. The RSPB has well over half a million members, and birds such as the capercaillie will not tolerate disturbance during the breeding season. Most visitors do keep to the paths as requested, but 'birders' are now so well educated that they have lists of even the rarest wildlife; they want to see it all, not just birds and mammals, but flowers and insects. The RSPB have many imaginative ways of showing wildlife to the public, not least at nearby Loch Garten Reserve, where well over a million people have enjoyed watching ospreys nesting, with no ill effect to the birds. Abernethy has many sensitive species which must come before people, so publicity will be limited to avoid the ultimate step of restricted access and special sanctuary areas.

However, human pressure causes little damage compared to over-grazing by deer. Indeed, people can be beneficial, for they disturb the deer and leave

This is how the forest has been since the Ice Age shaped these hills.

Rothiemurchus is visited by 500,000 people each year, so as to avoid damage and disturbance, education has become a priority.

It will take time, perhaps 200 years, for regeneration will be by purely natural means and though the plantations will be managed - as at Garten Wood - in the natural forest there will be no planting or fencing, no felling or thinning. This will ensure that Abernethy continues to be one of the finest examples of truly native woodland in Britain.

Other landowners are also looking for a dynamic and expanding native forest, and one of the most enlightened is John Grant of Rothiemurchus. For him, the greatest threat to the forest is fire, and his rangers are constantly alert to the problem. Rothiemurchus is visited by 500,000 thousand people each year, and even if only a tiny percentage cause problems or stray off the tracks, the damage and disturbance to wildlife can be considerable. In such circumstances education becomes a priority, and he provides an information centre, free film shows and ranger naturalists as guides.

human scent, discouraging grazing of young trees close to the footpaths. As a result the most popular walks are lined with dense areas of regeneration - encouragement for the future.

Elsewhere there are only patchy areas of regeneration - in some areas none at all - and if red deer are not reduced, the forests will become graveyards, each dead tree a symbol of man's short-sightedness. So the RSPB now has a policy of reducing deer to a number that the forest is able to sustain. Careful counts are carried out, avoiding the times when birds are nesting, and appropriate culling takes place in the autumn and winter.

The RSPB's intentions are ambitious, for they are not only going to encourage regeneration, including the broadleaf element, but hope to increase the extent of the forest from 4,000 to 12,000 acres, right up to the natural tree-line, a scale of management never attempted before in the history of British conservation.

Regeneration is John's other major concern, so deer management and fencing are an expensive necessity. Pine trees are not just beautiful but useful. They are one of the country's renewable natural resources and despite being a viable economic proposition are too often taken for granted. However, new attitudes and policies may in time provide incentives to landowners to improve regeneration and extend their forests.

The aims of the Forestry Commission's recent Pinewood Grant Scheme - to conserve existing native pinewoods and encourage their expansion - are welcomed by both the NCC and the RSPB, but they see snags. First, the timber production objective is mandatory, so the Government pays only for planting or regeneration. Second, there are no positive incentives for the continuing management of existing woodlands, which could mean that a woodland owner who incorporates nature conservation objectives could receive less grant. This is hardly likely to encourage them to approach the scheme with any enthusiasm. Above all, there is no incentive to leave the forests to grow naturally on their own - a sad reflection of the value we place on even our richest wild habitats.

The concern of one warden is that the Forestry Commission seem to be wanting owners to manage their woodland regardless of whether it is prime habitat or not, when the ideal scheme would provide both incentives to manage and, where appropriate, incentives to leave the forest alone. It is also the wish of many that the Forestry Commission attempt to correct past mistakes in woods of their ownership - which means removing exotic conifers from areas of ancient forest and ensuring the future of all the native pinewood remnants in their care.

Luckily, attitudes towards the Great Wood *are* improving. The forests are now looked at for their aesthetic appeal and their value to wildlife, as well as their commercial possibilities. Most of the remaining forest areas are now protected by sympathetic landowners, conservation organizations, and improved forestry policies, so the future is promising.

One day, perhaps, there will be a land-use policy for Scotland in which the primary use of the remaining native pinewoods *is* nature conservation. Roy Dennis, the RSPB's Highland Officer, believes Strathspey should have an advisory board to co-ordinate land-use, with each landowner providing a certain facility appropriate to his forest, instead of each trying to provide for all interests and risk destroying the wildlife. But he goes further than that. Roy has a dream that one day the forests of Abernethy, Rothiemurchus, Inshriach, Feshie and Kinveachy will grow to become one, that the Great Wood will rise again. It is a wildly ambitious dream but it is not impossible and, given the will, it can be achieved.

Adam Watson, one of the country's leading research biologists, is in no doubt about the importance of these magnificent native woodlands. 'These forests are unique in Europe, great natural monuments to an ancestral Caledonia, and must remain a priceless part of Scotland's heritage - a *living* heritage.'

Standing in the ancient forest as winter closed around us, we doubted that anyone sharing our experiences could question Adam's words of wisdom. The forest was alive, the trees still growing around us, as they had since the Ice Age shaped the hills. Snow clung to the veterans' craggy trunks and lay in thick blankets on their broad crowns. Their branches bowed but did not break. What was another winter to them? Some of these old giants had already endured two centuries of snow and ice, and would still be growing when we were gone. For some, this winter would be their last; but others would continue to reach up into the light and set their cones and provide a refuge for cat and squirrel and crested tit. It is an old story. The pines rise and fall but the Great Wood, though grievously reduced in size, lives on. It is perhaps the oldest living thing in Britain, and its native pines are among our most prized natural possessions. Like the oak, they have a courageous quality that sits well in their wild surroundings. Like the deer, their antlered shapes are symbols of strength and endurance. Landseer was wrong. It is the Scots pine, not the red stag, that is the true monarch of the glen.

Recommended Reading

Native Pine Woods in Scotland
Clifton Bain
Royal Society for the Protection of Birds (Edinburgh)

Native Pinewoods of Scotland
Proceedings of Aviemore Symposium 1975
R G H. Bunce and J N R Jeffers
Institute of Terrestrial Ecology

Plant Communities of the Scottish Highlands
D N McVean and D A Ratcliffe
HMSO

The Native Pinewoods of Scotland
H M Steven and A Carlisle

The Cairngorms
Desmond Nethersole-Thompson and Adam Watson
Collins

Pine Crossbills
Desmond Nethersole-Thompson
T & A D Poyser

Location of Landscape Photography